# POWER GAMES

## RITUAL AND RIVALRY
### AT THE
## ANCIENT GREEK OLYMPICS

# POWER GAMES

## RITUAL AND RIVALRY
### AT THE
## ANCIENT GREEK OLYMPICS

DAVID STUTTARD

THE BRITISH MUSEUM PRESS

*To the memory of my father, Philip*

© 2012 The Trustees of the British Museum

David Stuttard has asserted the right to be identified as the author of this work

First published in 2012 by The British Museum Press
A division of The British Museum Company Ltd
38 Russell Square
London WC1B 3QQ
britishmuseum.org/publishing

A catalogue record for this book is available from the British Library

ISBN: 978-0-7141-2272-4

Designed by Zoë Mellors
Printed in China by C&C Offset Printing Ltd

The majority of objects illustrated in this book are from the collection of the British Museum. The British Museum registration numbers for these objects are listed on page 237. You can find out more about objects in all areas of the British Museum collection on the Museum's website at britishmuseum.org.

*Front cover illustration* The horses pulling Hippolytus' chariot bolt (see page 89)
*Frontispiece* Greek decadrachm coin depicting a racing charioteer and Victory flying above. Engraved by Kimon. Silver, Syracuse, Sicily, 400–390 BC. Weight 43 g.

# CONTENTS

# INTRODUCTION

SPRING EQUINOX 416 BC

They had come to the hilltop to make sacrifice. Now, on this day of days when the world was balanced equally between light and darkness, the king-priests of Elis had climbed the wooded slopes above Olympia to make their offerings to Kronos, one of the most primeval and terrifying of all their gods. Legend told how, to preserve his power, Kronos had eaten his newborn children one by one, until at last Rhea, his wife, substituted a stone wrapped in swaddling clothes for her new baby. Kronos was

deceived. He swallowed Rhea's ruse, and so the child, Zeus, lived. In time Zeus overthrew his father and, with his siblings, now regurgitated and revitalized, he took the reins of power. But even defeated, the gods were chilling and must still be honoured, and that is why, on this first day of the new year, in the month known locally as the 'Month of the Deer', the priests had come to sacrifice and pray (no doubt) for a successful Games.

We know of this ceremony from a brief aside in an ancient travel book,[1] which throws up more questions than it answers: Who were these king-priests? What did they sacrifice? Was the ritual carried out in daylight or at night-time? What did they believe to be its purpose? About all these it is silent. Nonetheless, it does at least do one important thing: it reminds us how alien the world of antiquity was from our own.

There is a common (and understandable) tendency to draw parallels between antiquity and now, to see a pattern which repeats itself; to narrow the gulf between ancient and modern. In this way, we understand the classical past in terms of our own experience. There is much to be said for this approach. The way in which human beings respond to life-changing events has probably not changed much in the last two and a half thousand years: sorrow at the death of a loved one or joy at an unexpected

1. *The Hill of Kronos rises above the site of Olympia. Every year on the Spring Equinox, the king-priests of Elis made sacrifice on its summit.*

2. *The fertile valley of the River Kladeos stretching north from Olympia. In 416 BC, the whole area was controlled by the city of Elis.*

reunion. But how we in the West understand the world has changed enormously in ways too many and too obvious to list. New religions and technologies have all played their part in carrying us further and further away from the mindset of the ancient Greek.

Yet, like us, the ancient Greeks had their Olympic Games and there remains a compelling desire somehow to draw as many links as possible between the two. After all, is not the Olympic flame still lit at Olympia itself? Well, yes – but the lighting of the flame

was not part of the ancient Games. It was, in fact, invented as a piece of flummery for a certain Adolf Hitler by Leni Riefenstahl, who thought it would look good in the movie she was making of the 1936 Games in Berlin. And the Olympic ideals of amateurism? Dreamt up by a Frenchman in the nineteenth century, and inspired by the sports fields of the English public school. The modern revival of the Games has been well considered elsewhere.[2] Perhaps we might be better to call them 're-inventions'.

Even in antiquity the Olympic Games were constantly evolving. Over 500 years after the traditional date of their inauguration (in 776 BC) new events were still being added – and in the 500 years after that, the character of the Games was still being transformed. Conquering generals, megalomaniac Roman emperors and proselytizing Christians all saw to that. So, to talk of 'the ancient Olympic Games' as if they remained one and the same festival for over a millennium is almost as misleading as it is to think that they bore much similarity to our own athletic meetings.

For that reason, this book focuses on one Olympic Games, the Festival of 416 BC. As we shall see, this was a period of great uncertainty. Much of the Greek world, spread out as it was across most of the Mediterranean – from Marseilles in France to Miletus in Anatolia (now modern Turkey) – was (or was about to be) embroiled in war. Internally, some states were experiencing tensions between the many, who supported democracy, and rich aristocrats, who preferred oligarchic government. Internationally, alliances were being forged or broken, with policy being made either in great popular assemblies or in secret meetings between powerful politicians. The venue where such meetings could most easily be held, because it was here that for a few days there was the highest concentration of such politicians, was the Olympic Games. We shall see how one politician in particular, Alcibiades of Athens, used the Games of 416 BC both to enhance his prestige and to consolidate his power, and, following his subsequent career, we shall trace the increasingly disastrous course of the years immediately following.

That the Games were not all about athletics should not come as a great surprise. What is more alien to us is that they were, in fact, only one aspect of a much greater festival dominated by a religious ritual centred on the second or third full moon after the summer solstice.[3] By 416 BC this four-yearly Olympic Festival, with its focus on the Temple of Zeus and its great statue (one of the wonders of the ancient world), had become the most significant religious event in the panhellenic (Greek) calendar, something to which people flocked in their tens of thousands from all over the Greek-speaking world. The closest (but still wildly dissimilar) modern parallel is perhaps the annual Hajj pilgrimage to Mecca.

Olympia itself was exclusively a religious sanctuary. There was no town or village here, only a sacred enclosure, the Altis, with its temples, shrines and statues, on a fertile plain below the wooded Hill of Kronos, where two rivers met. For most of the time it was peaceful and relatively deserted. Then, once every four years in the height of summer, it became a chaotic melee as athletes and trainers, delegates, spectators and speculators, selling everything from souvenirs to sausages, descended for a noisome few days, and then went away again.[4]

Much was crammed into those five or six days: processions; banquets; animal sacrifices on a quite industrial scale; sightseeing; deal-making; hymn-singing; celebrity-watching; philosophizing; speechifying; literary readings; and (for a few hours each day) a sporting event or two.

This book seeks to put those sporting events into context – both the context of the Festival itself and the wider social and political context of the time – though space will not permit consideration of the other festivals at which athletes from Greek cities competed. These were the Games held at Nemea, Delphi and Corinth,[5] which joined with those at Olympia to form a regular circuit.

We do not know precisely how the Games were organized and the order of events is controversial, so care has been taken to identify what in this account is fact and what is speculation. By rooting itself firmly in one specific year, the book aims to recreate something of the experience of attending the Festival of 416 BC. But its scope does not confine itself to this one year. Using references to other Games both earlier and later, it endeavours to present the Festival as part of a continuum – an event which linked not only one city to another but one generation to the next; a contest in which every man from every state and every age was striving to be the best.

Perhaps no one was more aware of this than the king-priests as they carried out their mysterious rites on the summit of the fragrant Hill of Kronos. After all, had Kronos himself not been defeated by his own son Zeus, the power of the old king giving way to that of the new? As they made their short descent, leaving behind whatever offerings they had made, they would have entered the sacred enclosure, the Altis, described by many who visited as having a unique atmosphere of divinity.[6] Down past the terrace of the treasuries; past the Temple of Hera, with its squat columns, some of wood, some now of stone; then skirting round the Temple of Zeus, completed already a generation earlier, its great statue still enough to send a frisson up the spine; a pause perhaps to glance up at the new Victory, frozen as she swooped down from the sky on eagle-back; and so on to the Bouleuterion, the administrative centre of Olympia. For the Games were now only five months away. And there was much to do.

CHAPTER 1

# ZEUS, THE BEARER
# OF VICTORY

FULL MOON MINUS 14 (THE DAY OF THE NEW MOON)

It must have seemed that they had come into the presence of
pure molten power.[7] For, as the priests and temple wardens,
each clutching an urn of scented olive oil, passed between the
great bronze-plated doors, through from the dazzling high
summer sunlight to the awesome, darkened, echoing interior,
they saw ahead of them a god. And not just a minor god at that.
Towering massively above them, raised on a platform and seated
on a gilded and elaborately carved chair, his golden robes
shimmering, his ivory skin glowing with supernal life, was
enthroned the strongest and most powerful god of all: Olympian
Zeus. Here was the ruler of the earth and sky, the god of Justice,
god of gods, the god to whom this sanctuary was dedicated, and
from whom it took its name: Olympia.[8]

Already, over three Olympiads before,[9] Zeus had sent a sign
that the statue, on which the wardens and the priests were gazing,
pleased him. When its sculptor, Pheidias, had finished, he had
prayed to the god to indicate somehow if he approved of the
creation. Immediately a lightning bolt crashed down from heaven,
shattering part of the temple's marble paving. Awe-struck, the
priests had dedicated a bronze urn which stood now on the very spot
the lightning bolt had struck. Or so they liked to tell their visitors.[10]

Now, they approached the statue, their footsteps echoing on the

white marble floor. Halfway between the door and statue base they stopped. Here was the barrier, which ran around the whole statue, designed to keep sightseers out, and to enclose the area to which the wardens and the priests had come. Opening the gate, they all filed in and round the white marble walkway which defined the edge of a shallow pool. Then, perhaps after a prayer of dedication, they emptied their urns of viscous oil onto the black stone paving,[11] and the perfume of rose petals filled the air.[12]

They had been advised to do this by Pheidias himself. Olympia was marshy and the oil would protect the statue's wooden infrastructure from harm.[13] Moreover, there were said to be tiny channels leading from the pool into the sculpture's base, from where the oil was drawn up and into the very core of the statue.

The sanctuary was still quiet. None of the raucous crowds had yet arrived for the great Festival, and the athletes were in training forty miles away in Elis. So, now that their ritual was done, the priests perhaps could take time to look once more upon the statue of the god and marvel.

It was indeed an awe-inspiring sight. Later generations would list the statue as one of the seven wonders of the world. Our best description comes from Pausanias, a traveller in the second century AD (some five and a half centuries after its creation), whose accounts of his observations at Olympia are invaluable. Originally from Lydia in modern Turkey, Pausanias travelled widely throughout Greece, inspecting sites and works of art, interviewing everyone he could, from local experts to garrulous

3. *Modern reconstruction of Pheidias' gold and ivory statue of Zeus as it may have appeared in the temple at Olympia in 416 BC. Polyurethane resin with details picked out with gilding and acrylic paint. Height 50 cm (scale 1:25). British Museum. Made by Sophie Kleinschmidt, the reconstruction was researched and supervised by Judith Swaddling in 2008.*

old men, and recording his findings in the ten books of his *Periegesis,* his *'Guide to Greece'*. He began writing in the reign of the emperor Hadrian (r. AD 117–138), whose own building programme in Greece was energetic and ambitious to say the least. But for Pausanias, nowhere compared to Olympia,[14] and nothing to the great statue of Zeus. His is an eyewitness description:

> The god, who sits on a throne, is made of gold and ivory.
> He wears a wreath on his head crafted to resemble the leaves
> and twigs of olive. In his right hand he holds Victory, also
> made of ivory and gold, with a ribbon in her hands and a
> garland on her head. In the god's left hand is a sceptre
> wound with flowers made from every kind of metal, and the
> bird perching on the sceptre is the eagle. The god's sandals
> and robes are also made of gold, and his robes are inlaid with
> signs of the zodiac[15] and lilies in full flower. Part of the
> throne is made of gold studded with gemstones, part of
> ebony and ivory: on it there are paintings of animals and

4. *Modern model showing (centre) the painted and gilded Temple of Zeus with the workshop of Pheidias behind it to the left. The view is from the south-east.*

---

carvings of figures. Four Victories are dancing on each of the four feet of the throne, and two others dance beneath each foot ... On the highest part of the throne, above the head of the statue, Pheidias has crafted the Graces and the Seasons, three of each ... On the footstool there are golden sculptures of lions ... On the platform supporting the throne and the statue of Zeus with all its many decorations there are figures of gold ...[16]

The statue was over thirteen metres tall. So much ivory, imported from both Africa and India, was used to represent the god's flesh that one visitor exclaimed that it must have been for this alone that nature had invented elephants. Another, the philosopher Epictetus, an older contemporary of Pausanias, recorded that 'the Zeus at Olympia does not frown haughtily at you. Rather, he fixes you with his eyes as is proper for one who says: "what I have decreed cannot be revoked and it will come to pass."'[17] He added: 'You journey to Olympia to gaze on the statue of Zeus, and every one of you would think it a great misfortune to die never having seen it.'[18]

But (as the priests in the temple knew full well) for all its spiritual impact, the making of the statue of Zeus had been inexorably tied up with the politics of Olympia. In 471 BC, after a brief but bloody war, the new democracy of Elis had wrested control of the sanctuary and Games from her close neighbour, Pisa, looting her defeated enemy's city and lands. To mark the victory, and with the booty won from it, the Eleans (the people of Elis) had commissioned a local architect, Libon, to design and build an impressive Temple of Zeus at Olympia. Eight years after the first stone was laid, the temple was complete (458 BC), but it would be some two decades before work on the statue was begun.

5. *Persian warriors on parade. Limestone relief, Achaemenid, Six–fifth century BC. Width 106 cm; height 51 cm. Donated by Sir Gore Ouseley.*

By then, the sculptor with the greatest reputation throughout the Greek-speaking world was an Athenian, Pheidias. He had already made his mark in his home city with his great statue of Athene, housed in her new temple, the Parthenon. Of a similar height to that of the Zeus at Olympia, the statue of Athene was also faced with gold and ivory. She, too, held a Victory in her outstretched hand. She, too, had been erected from the spoils of war.

Wars and victory, ivory and gold: it is time for us to pause, and, like the priests, to consider some of the events of the previous three generations, and how they shaped the Greek world. In this way, we might begin to understand the tensions, the alliances, the ambitions and suspicions which suffused these pivotal Olympic Games of 416 BC.

In 490 BC, the city-states of mainland Greece had faced destruction. The Persian Empire had already swallowed up a constellation of Greek-founded cities like Miletus and Ephesus on its western sea-board (modern Turkey), and now it was looking across the Aegean Sea to Greece itself. Darius, the Persian 'Great King' (r. 522–486 BC), was irritated by Athens and the Greek island of Euboia, which had both lent support to rebels in Miletus, and he vowed to punish them. But against all odds, the expedition he sent out was defeated on the plain of Marathon. Heavily outnumbered though they were, the hoplite soldiers[19] of Athens and Plataea overpowered the Persian invaders, who scrambled hastily into their ships and fled. For now, the mainland city-states were free. So, the people of Athens raised a grave-mound for their dead, and began the process of turning them into heroes. Miltiades, their general, dedicated his war helmet as a thanks-offering to Zeus at Olympia.[20]

Ten years later, and the Persians were back. This time it

looked as if there would be no stopping them. With Darius dead, it fell to Xerxes, his son and successor (r. 486–465 BC), to complete the work he had begun. So, with the hardened general Mardonius riding at their head, troops drawn from every corner of the sprawling Persian empire crossed the Bosphorus strait on a bridge of boats and headed west and south for Athens, while a great navy hugged the coast and shadowed them. At the narrow pass of Thermopylae their advance was briefly checked – in the final hours by 300 Spartan warriors, keen to make up for their absence from Marathon ten years before, when they had missed the battle because they were observing a religious festival. But even the Spartans could not hold back the Persian juggernaut, and, on the same day as Thermopylae fell, the Athenian fleet fled from its forward base at Artemisium. The road to Athens was now clear, and it was

6. *At Thermopylae, the sheer number of arrows fired by Persian archers, such as the one depicted here, were said to block out the sun. Red-figure pottery, Athens, 520–510 BC. Diameter 19.5 cm.*

not long before the Persians were inside the city and the temples
on the Acropolis were torched.

Those cities that were still free held a hurried conference. Most
wished to fortify the narrow isthmus near Corinth, the only land-
bridge leading to the south, the Peloponnese. But the Athenians
had not yet given up. In a desperate bid, their general
Themistocles tricked the Persians into joining battle in the straits
of Salamis, between the island and the coast. So confident was
Xerxes, that he had a golden throne placed high on the headland
overlooking Salamis, that he might savour what he felt certain
would be victory. He was mistaken. His fleet was decimated and
his army forced to withdraw. In one final battle, the city-states of
Greece, now for the first time united, defeated Mardonius and his
army at Plataea. Left on the battlefield, amid the corpses of so
many Persian dead was Xerxes' lavish tent,[21] a symbol to the
Greeks of their would-be ruler's empty vanity. From the spoils of
war, they forged a golden tripod supported by a bronze serpent
with three heads, and dedicated it to Apollo, son of Zeus, at the
sanctuary at Delphi. When the accompanying inscription was
eventually agreed, it recorded the names of all the cities which
had fought in the wars against the Persians. For a brief moment,
the Greeks had united against a common enemy and been
victorious, and when next Themistocles appeared at the Olympic
Games the spectators broke into such wildly enthusiastic applause
that proceedings had temporarily to be suspended.

But despite their common heritage, this unity was not to last.
Within a few years, the Greeks had liberated the occupied cities
on the eastern Aegean coastline, but already their alliance had
fragmented. As a maritime state with interests to the east, it was
to Athens' advantage to ensure the cooperation of the islands and
the city-states of the Aegean. So, with Sparta and the other major

mainland powers, like Thebes and Corinth, whose interests lay elsewhere, losing interest in maintaining sufficient troops abroad to ensure security against the Persians, Athens took the lead. A year after the battle of Plataea, she and many of the Aegean states established an alliance (478 BC), with its treasury on the sacred island of Delos. Its purpose: to protect its members from the Persian threat.

In theory, each member of this so-called 'Delian League' was supposed to contribute its share of ships and crew, but many soon preferred to make an annual cash payment and allow Athens to provide protection from her growing fleet. Bit by bit the balance of power changed. Even before a peace treaty was made with the Persians, some of the islanders, who tried to leave the alliance, found their harbours occupied by an imperious Athenian fleet and

their independence gone. In opposing the Persian Empire, they had sleep-walked into a new empire ruled by Athens.

At the same time, tensions between Athens and the rest of Greece were growing. Things came to a head in 462 BC. When the Spartans' Helot slaves[22] rose up against their masters, the Athenians sent 4,000 hoplites south to Messenia to help quell the rebellion. But the Spartans, always anxious about homeland security, sent the Athenians home, accusing them of encouraging revolution among the very slaves they were supposed to be subduing. It was an episode from which relations between the two states would not recover.

---

7. *The rebuilding of temples on Athens' Acropolis celebrated the end of the war with Persia and demonstrated the power of the growing Athenian Empire.*

Peace with the Persians (449 BC) allowed Athens to use the taxes from her growing empire for projects other than defence. One of the most significant was the rebuilding of the temples on the Acropolis, which had been destroyed by Xerxes' army. Under the direction of Pericles – the effective 'first citizen' of Athens and himself nick-named 'Olympian' because of his Zeus-like power and wisdom – the Athenians entered on an ambitious building project. The undoubted jewel in its crown was the temple of Athene the Virgin (Parthenos), the Parthenon. As artistic director of the entire project, Pericles appointed Pheidias, whose sculptures had already won him great renown. Since his remit meant that he was responsible not only for the cult statue of

Athene but for the sculptures on the building too, Pheidias was able to ensure that the iconography of all the artwork was thematically linked in a way which had never before been attempted. Thus, the sculptures depicted not only the triumph of civilization over barbarism (a non-so-subtle code for the victory of Greece over Persia) but the future glory of Athens itself.[23]

The dedication of the Parthenon in 438 BC meant that Pheidias was free to accept other commissions, and it was now that he was invited to Olympia to create his masterwork, the statue of Zeus, Bearer of Victory. It was a colossal undertaking. First, Pheidias insisted on the building of his workshop in an exact alignment with the temple's *cella* (or nave) in which the statue was to sit; a

8. *The workshop of Pheidias today. It was built to the same dimensions as the cella of the temple, which would house the finished statue of Zeus.*

replica in every way but for a series of windows high up in the side walls, which could be unshuttered while he worked to let in the light. While this building was being constructed, there were the materials to order: cedar wood for the throne, ebony and precious jewels with which to decorate the robes, gold to be hammered into easily-worked leaf, ivory tusks to be carefully unscrolled and flattened into thin strips, then treated with an arcane compound of chemicals, ready to be moulded.[24]

No doubt surrounded by a willing team of apprentices and

assistants, some sawing wood at benches, some firing clay moulds for bronze-casting, some stoking furnaces for the multitude of glass stars and palm leaves which would adorn the golden drapery,[25] Pheidias strained and sweated in his workshop to produce his masterpiece. During periods of intense effort, the whole team ate, drank and perhaps even slept on site. At some stage, the master sculptor, possessive of his crockery, even took time to engrave on the base of his own mug 'I belong to Pheidias'. Of course, it was not all work. In all probability, the statue was still under construction in the 86th Olympiad (of 436 BC), when Pheidias' young lover, a local boy, Pantarkes of Elis, won the wrestling match for youths. A legend soon grew up that Pheidias had immortalized him on the statue's base as a young man tying a victory ribbon round his head.[26]

Like his statue of Athene in Athens, when Pheidias' Zeus was set in place, it would be suffused with a golden glow, for the roofs of the temples, in which each was housed, were made of the thinnest marble, translucent, allowing daylight to filter subtly through; a honeyed radiance which enhanced their aura of divinity. Like his Athene statue, too, his Zeus was constructed in such a way that it could be dismantled and reformed. This was essential, as eventually it had to be transported from the workshop to the temple. At last, it was in place, and the finishing details could be added: the colouring of the ivory so that it more closely resembled human flesh; the painting of the animals on the wooden throne; the fixing of the glass and jewels to the robe. Assisting Pheidias in all this was his brother, Panainos,[27] himself a celebrated painter, whose fresco depiction of the Battle of Marathon in the Painted Stoa in Athens had attracted loud praise.[28]

But that was nothing compared to the praise accorded Pheidias' Zeus. It was the sublime expression of the god which most caught the imagination. How had the sculptor managed it, they asked? Had he been transported up to Mount Olympus itself; had he gazed upon the true face of the god? Pheidias' response was to quote three lines of Homer's *Iliad*, which he claimed had inspired him:

> Zeus, the son of Kronos, spoke, and he inclined his head with its dark brows,
> And the mighty king's hair, anointed with ambrosial oil,
> Fell forward from his immortal head; and great Olympus trembled.[29]

Only the olive wreath which encircled the god's dark-blue painted locks was not in Homer. Pheidias had added this for a specific reason: it was the prize striven for by every athlete at the Games; the sacred symbol of the greatest victory. And now here, for the first time, Zeus himself proudly wore it, too, even as Victory herself danced on his outstretched hand.

But for all he had created a monument to power and awe, Pheidias could not resist one intensely personal romantic gesture: engraved, but hidden on Zeus' little finger was said to be the name of the sculptor's lover, 'handsome Pantarkes'.[30] Proud on the base for all to see, the legend: 'Pheidias the son of Charmides from Athens made me'.[31]

The statue of the king of all the Greek gods was now in place in the great panhellenic sanctuary, Olympia. But no sooner was the statue dedicated, at the end of the 430s BC, than the Greek world was again under threat – and this time, the threat came not from outside, but from within.

Ever since the showdown in Messenia (see pp. 23–4), relations between Athens and Sparta had been worsening. Now, in 431 BC,

they erupted into all-out war. A disagreement over a far-off city-state[32] had brought Athens into conflict with her trading rival, Corinth. At the same time, Athens' imposition of harsh economic sanctions on neighbouring Megara was seen as an unfair act of gross high-handedness. Hostilities ensued. A coalition of independent city-states opposed to Athens formed a confederacy under the leadership of Sparta. The so-called Peloponnesian War[33] had begun.

From the outset, it was brutal, and, as the years went by and more and more atrocities were committed, it seemed set to change the face not only of warfare but of acceptable morality. Moreover, natural forces conspired with man-made cruelty to ensure that from the start the body count was high. In the second year of the war (429 BC) a plague, now thought to be typhoid fever,[34] broke out in Egypt, whence it was carried swiftly on warships and transport boats to Athens. Here it found the urban population swollen by their country cousins, all crammed inside

9. *Zeus enthroned (right) with his wife Hera beside him.*
*Designed by Pheidias, this relief sculpture from the*
*Parthenon Frieze suggests the majesty of his statue of Zeus*
*at Olympia. Marble, Athens, 447–432 BC. Height 99 cm.*

the safety of the walls to escape Spartan raids. The effect was devastating. An estimated third of the entire population died. Among them was Pericles, the main driving force behind the war and its chief strategist.

Despite the horrors of the plague, the war dragged on, with now one side then the other seeming to be on the brink of victory. The turning point came unexpectedly. In 425 BC, an Athenian fleet, sailing round the southern Peloponnese was forced by a storm to put in to shore at Pylos, deep in the Helot country of Messenia. The Athenian commander seized the opportunity, hurriedly building a fort from which he hoped to stir up insurrection among the Spartans' Helot slaves. After a summer of nail-biting moves and countermoves, over 400 Spartan soldiers, who had taken up position on an island opposite the fort, were cut off by the Athenian navy. 120 of the Spartan elite were taken prisoner. It was the first time in their history that the Spartans had surrendered. Not only were they seized with an almost overwhelming sense of shame, a significant proportion of Sparta's fighting force was now being held in Athens as prisoners-of-war – a significant bargaining chip when it came to terms for peace. In the early spring of 421 BC a treaty, the so-called Peace of Nikias, was signed, effectively allowing both sides to return to the status quo which had prevailed before the war began. Ten years of fighting had resulted in nothing.

Or not quite nothing. Across Greece and the Aegean there were physical signs everywhere of battles won and lost – trophies set up by victorious armies over their defeated enemies. One of the most spectacular of these had been raised at Olympia itself. To commemorate their part in the defeat of the Spartans at Pylos, the people of Messenia had commissioned a statue of Victory from the sculptor Paionios of Mende,[35] who years before had worked on the sculptures on the eastern pediment of Zeus' temple. Completed and dedicated in the years immediately following the signing of the peace treaty, the Victory was truly wondrous. Raised on top of a tapering triangular pillar, almost ten metres above the ground, it was positioned about thirty metres east of the entrance to the Temple of Zeus, and dominated the approach to it. Victory herself, winged and in flowing robes of scarlet; her black curls encircled in a golden band; her left breast naked; her left arm upraised; was borne aloft on the back of an eagle, the sacred bird of Zeus. In her right hand, she held a palm branch, in her left an olive crown. What was most remarkable was the illusion of movement which Paionios had achieved. It seemed that both eagle and Victory were swooping down to earth to land at the very doors of the temple and gaze inside at that other Victory poised on Zeus' outstretched hand. But what each of the Victories symbolized was very different: the one in the temple spoke of victory in the Games; the other, on eagle-back, of victory hard-won in battle. Whenever a Spartan came to Olympia, he would look on Paionios' sculpture and remember his city's defeat.

Of course, feelings of hostility cannot be ended by the signing of a treaty, and new tensions can quickly arise. Weeks after the sacrifices had been made to ratify the Peace of Nikias (March 421 BC), the cities of Triphylia, an area just south of Olympia, staged a revolt against Elis, by which they had been ruled for over four centuries. The revolt was supported by Sparta, much to the surprise of the Eleans, who had been strong and loyal allies of the Spartans for many years. The Eleans quickly formed a new alliance – this time with Athens. Passions boiled on all sides, and to underline their anger, the Olympic authorities, based at Elis, issued a decree banning Sparta from competing in the coming

Games of 420 BC.[36] Conveniently for Elis, the Spartans had seized the nearby town of Lepreum during the period of the Sacred Truce, which apparently forbade participating states to go to war.[37] No doubt with a wry smile, the Elean officials could argue that Sparta had effectively disqualified herself.

The atmosphere throughout these Games was tense to say the least. Throughout the tented settlement of athletes and spectators, delegates and marketeers, speculation ran rife that the Spartan army might appear at any moment to wreak its revenge. In the end, there was indeed a Spartan intervention, but a curious and unexpected one. On the second day of the competition, the chariot race was won by a team entered in the name of the city of Thebes. But, when its owner stepped forward to tie the victor's ribbon round the head of the winning charioteer, there was a sharp intake of breath. For the owner was a Spartan, Likhas, an elderly aristocrat, one of Sparta's ruling council. With the connivance of her close ally Thebes, Sparta had clearly flouted the ban. The Olympic judges were incensed. They seized Likhas and, with no concern for his age or status, stripped him of his clothes, whipped him and flung him, bruised and bleeding, out of the enclosure. It was an episode which would not be forgotten – and not least by the Spartans. They nursed their wrath for twenty years and then took their revenge (see p. 203).

Interventions in alliances, the ferment of revolt and discontent in minor states and cities: this was the treaty's aftermath, a phony cold war waged by politicians on all sides who knew that it was but a matter of time before hostilities broke out again. For some

10. Smouldering good looks: this Roman mosaic of Athenian playboy, politician and general Alcibiades conveys something of his personality, if not his exact appearance. Archaeological Museum of Sparta, Greece.

of them, it seemed that war could not come soon enough. In Athens, in particular, there was a new breed of firebrand demagogues, ready to play on the people's memories of past victories at Marathon and Salamis to whip up patriotic zeal. Chief among these was the super-rich *wunderkind* Alcibiades (fig. 10), now in his early 30s, ward of the statesman Pericles, but as unlike Pericles as it was possible to be.

Orphaned as a child, Alcibiades had inherited a fortune. He knew how to use it. In democratic Athens, where public recognition was key to gaining power, he made sure that his name was on everybody's lips. Stories soon multiplied of how he had appeared in the market, dressed in sumptuous robes, which he ostentatiously allowed to trail in the filth and ordure of the busy lanes until they were quite ruined[38] – or of the expensive hunting dog, whose tail he lopped off to the horror of his fellow citizens. When a friend berated him, saying that all Athens was outraged at his actions, his answer was: 'Good. Just what I wanted. They're talking about me.'[39] As well as wealth, Alcibiades possessed smouldering good looks. Again, he knew how to use them. Athenian society being what it was, he was soon being fought over by some of the most influential men in the city. Alcibiades chose his lovers well, knowing how best to manipulate each one the most successfully to further his career. Only the philosopher Socrates is said to have been able to resist him,

11. *The terrace of the twelve treasuries of the Dorian Greeks as it looks today, with columns from the Temple of Hera in the background (left).*

though in the end the two men's fates would be inexorably linked (see p. 201). At the same time, Alcibiades courted ties with powerful foreign cities, not least the rich commercial centres of the eastern Aegean, strategic entrepôts like Ephesus and prosperous island states like Chios and Lesbos. Monitoring his rise to power, they all responded.

Now, as the 91st Olympiad of 416 BC approached, Alcibiades

felt the time had come to flex his political muscles. He had
already double-crossed a Spartan delegation sent to Athens to
clarify some of the terms of the Peace of Nikias, causing them to
be belittled in front of the Popular Assembly. Now, with Sparta's
humiliating treatment at the Olympic Games fresh in everybody's
minds, he moved to cement a new alliance which included not
only Athens and Elis but the powerful Peloponnesian states of
Argos and Achaia. Bit by bit, they baited Sparta, chipping away at
her power base, making treaties and then immediately breaking

12. *The Treasury of Sikyon today. In 416 BC, it was crammed with breathtaking riches, a tantalizing glimpse of the wealth of Greek Sicily.*

them, goading them until at last, in a pitched battle on the plain at Mantineia (418 BC), Sparta once more proved her mettle and defeated them. For Alcibiades, it was a minor setback. His horizons were widening. Already, by the Olympiad of 416 BC, he was secretly planning the most ambitious military campaign that Athens had ever launched: the invasion of Sicily.

Sicily and southern Italy, the northern coast of Africa and the south coast of France – all had been colonized over two centuries before by the city-states of mainland Greece, and many had grown rich. At Olympia itself, some had their treasuries. The priests and wardens knew them well, the row of twelve neat buildings, some the size of temples, which stretched, shimmering in the sun, across the northern terrace of the sanctuary. They knew, too, of the breathtaking riches they contained. And they knew that all of them, the Treasuries of Sikyon and Gela, of Sybaris and Syracuse and all the rest, had been set up by Dorians, Greek peoples ethnically related to the Spartans. Alcibiades knew too. He had, of course, already visited Olympia more than once. For him, the Treasuries were but a foretaste of the wealth which might be his.

Of course, for now, Alcibiades' plans were classified. The priests and wardens knew nothing of them. But they might have heard disturbing news from one of the Aegean islands. Melos had so far resisted taking sides. Despite being Dorian, it had refrained from entering the Spartan confederacy; nor had it become part of Athens' empire. But now all that was about to change. A delegation had arrived from Athens with an ultimatum: pay tribute to us or accept the consequences. When the islanders objected saying that this was unjust, the argument came back that justice lay in power. Athens had expressed her new philosophy: if you were not for her, you were against her. Might was right.

Perhaps by now, reports had reached Olympia of how the Athenian fleet had put in at the harbour of Melos and how the city was already under siege.

Whatever they had heard, as they turned to leave the temple for the summer birdsong of the sanctuary outside, the priests and wardens would have felt that times were changing. No doubt they argued about whether it was Zeus or man who was responsible. But in the end they had more pressing things to think about: it was only a few days until the first of the vast crowds arrived. There were even rumours that the citizens of Ephesus were meaning to erect a silken tent, accommodation for their hero Alcibiades – a tent, some muttered, not unlike the tent the Persians had left behind when they fled from Plataea. There were so many rumours, and so much for the authorities to organize; so much that seemed immediately so pressing. How could they know that the fall-out from the coming Festival would very nearly tear the whole Greek world apart?

CHAPTER 2

# ARRIVAL, POMP, CEREMONY AND CONFLICT

## DAY 1 (FULL MOON MINUS TWO)

Olympia had been transformed. In the past days, the trickle of those pitching tents on the plain outside the Altis had become a torrent, and now it seemed that there was scarcely room for more.

As the priests had predicted, the prime place had been appropriated by a delegation from Ephesus who had taken care to arrive in good time to set up the most elaborate dwelling yet seen at Olympia – a construction which threatened to eclipse in spectacle even the Temple of Zeus. The word 'tent' could scarcely describe it. With its costly hangings and its priceless furnishing, its richly woven carpets and its cushions soft as down, its ornately carved and tight-strung bed frames, its gauzy curtains and its tables piled with gold, it was in all but name a royal pavilion.[40] Ephesus, the richest city in the east was paying lavish homage to the rising star of Athens: Alcibiades. Around the pavilion were other sumptuous tents, each opulent and some flamboyant, symbols of the wealth of families from the islands or Ionia; land-owners, merchants, mining moguls, all vying to be seen as vital players in the new Athenian empire.

Elsewhere, in the Dorian encampment, were the Spartan tents. These were as ostentatious as Alcibiades' pavilion, but in their own and opposite way. Spartans took pride in austerity. No beds for them – only hard earth. No gourmandizing meals – only their infamous black broth. Theirs was a single-mindedness which brooked no levity. Life's sole purpose was the survival of Sparta. At any personal cost. Although the other Dorian states and Sparta's allies undoubtedly admired her, they felt no need to subject themselves to such rigours. The men of Sicily,

sophisticates from Syracuse and Acragas and Gela, must have felt more at ease with perfumed Corinthians than with the battle-scarred warriors from the Eurotas valley.[41]

Time and custom had no doubt established a tradition of where each city pitched its tents, although shifting alliances must have led to a certain fluidity. Equally, there must have been some form of hierarchy which dictated where the rich encamped, and where the poor. For many of the thousands who had turned up at Olympia this year, as every other year, were there not so much to observe the Festival as to make as much money as they could in the short time available. Everyone from fast-food vendors to jugglers, from buskers to bric-a-brac merchants, from fortune-tellers to sellers of cheap souvenirs and even (no doubt) from drug dealers[42] to pre-pubescent slave-girls sold for sex, all crammed in their cramped tatty tents with an eye to the main chance. (Only married women were banned from the Festival, which in effect meant any woman past the age of puberty.[43]) By the last day of the Festival, conditions in the campsite must have been unpleasant to say the least. Water was at a premium. Apart from the nearby River Alpheios, which flows all year round, there

13. *Like Ephesus, the island of Lesbos, seen across the sea through the columns of the Temple of Athene at Assos, feted Alcibiades at the Games of 416 BC.*

were only nine fountains fed by underground channels[44] and a few
specially-dug wells. There was no sanitation and no facility for
bathing. In the heat of a Greek August, it is not hard to imagine
the resulting stench.

Five hundred years later (when the crowds were even greater),
even a Stoic like Epictetus would complain about 'the cacophony,
the din, the jostling, the shoving, the crowding and so many
people all doing something different'.[45] He enumerated the
discomforts: 'Are you not burnt by the sun? Are you not squashed
by the crowds? Can you get clean? Don't you get drenched when
it rains? Don't you have to endure noise and tumult and all the
other unpleasantness?' 'But', he went on to say, 'I think that you
are happy put up with all of this when you think of the splendour
of the spectacles.'[46]

The first of these spectacles had already occurred. A matter of
hours earlier, as the previous day ended with the setting of the
sun,[47] the procession of athletes had arrived at Olympia. For a
month, they had been billeted in Elis, nearly forty miles away.
Here, the athletes had been compelled to prove their eligibility to
take part in the Games, convincing the authorities somehow that
they were pure-blooded, free-born Greeks. Here they had been
obliged to train and compete in the initial heats under the strict
watch of the *Hellanodikai* (or 'Greek Judges' as they were
somewhat grandiloquently called).[48] Here, too, the fitness of the
athletes had been tested and decisions made as to who should
compete in which event.

Particularly difficult were the decisions concerning young men
of a certain (or rather, uncertain) age. Should they be entered in
events for men or for boys? The cut-off age was twenty, but, with
no supporting documentation, judges were occasionally forced to
make controversial decisions. Fifty years earlier at the 78th

Olympiad,[49] a certain Pherias from the island of Aegina (just opposite Athens) was prevented from taking part in the wrestling contest because he looked too young.[50] But the judges' rulings were not solely based on age. On another occasion, the hulking Nikasylos, from the Eastern Mediterranean island of Rhodes, was deemed so strong that he was entered in the men's wrestling event although he was only eighteen. What's more, he won – and he went on to win at both the Isthmian and the Nemean Games, though he died before he reached the age of twenty.[51]

For the Greeks, winning was everything. There was little, if any, sense of sporting camaraderie. The testosterone-fuelled egos of the athletes, most of whose city-states were likely to be at war

14. *A girl kneads dough for bread. With vast crowds of spectators at the Games, fast-food vendors must have hoped to make a good profit. Terracotta, Kamiros, Rhodes, c.450 BC. Height 12.7 cm.*

with at least one other, must have made the atmosphere of that month in Elis very tense indeed. Yet we hear of no ugly incidents. It was, perhaps, in no one's interest to record them. Ten months in all the athletes were obliged to train, the last of which was spent at Elis, and now that period was finally over. With two days to go, they had set out in a sacred procession for what they all hoped fervently would be the site of their great victory: Olympia.

Journeying as they did on foot, their procession resembled a pilgrimage. For every one of them it was an integral part of the Festival, something with which many would be familiar from similar processions in their home states.[52] By the end of the first day, they would have walked well over twenty miles. Behind them was the city, Elis, with its gymnasia and wrestling pits, its market square which had thundered to the rattle of the chariots and the hoof-thud of the horses as they trained; behind them its temples, shrines and statues – including an Athene[53] and an Aphrodite[54] both by Pheidias; behind them its towering ancient walls. So, the athletes and the *Hellanodikai* had struck out south along the Sacred Road towards Letrinoi and the sea. Their path took them first from the mountains to the plain and to the flatlands

15. *A pig goes to ritual sacrifice. On the eve of the Games, the Hellanodikai purified themselves in pig's blood. Bronze, Roman, first to second century AD. Height 10.2 cm.*

where fine flax was grown.[55] For a moment the peasants in the fields stopped their back-breaking work to watch the procession passing far off through the heat haze. Later, the athletes and judges paused by the Fountain of Piera beside the level road. Here a solemn sacrifice took place, the slaughter of a pig, with whose blood the *Hellanodikai* were smeared to purify them.[56] Then in the waters of the fountain they cleansed themselves of the steaming sticky gore.

That night, they all slept at Letrinoi near where the river Alpheios debouched into the sea. The association of the town with the sacred river of Olympia made it an obvious location for the pilgrims' rest. Legend told how Alpheios, the river's god, had once been struck with lust for Artemis, the virgin goddess of the wild. Knowing that she and the nymphs would come to Letrinoi to celebrate a festival, Alpheios hid in waiting. But Artemis was wise. She and her nymphs all plastered thick mud on their faces, so Alpheios did not know which she was. The river-god's lust was thwarted. But the people of Letrinoi worshipped Artemis particularly, calling her first Artemis of Alpheios (*Alpheiaia*), then Artemis of the Deer (*Elaphiaia*), the title under which the Eleans themselves paid honour to her.[57]

At daybreak, the procession set off once again, inland and west, the fifteen miles along the valley of the Alpheios with the cicadas' hoarse dry rasping ever louder in the rising heat until at last they reached Olympia. As news of their imminent arrival spread through the encampment, the crowds ran out to greet them: wrestlers and runners, riders, boxers, pankratists. As each man in the massing throng saw one from his own city, he would cheer the louder. So, as the athletes dispersed to tents or training, the sun sank, and the moon rose on the first day of the 91st Olympic Games.

It was the ideal time for many to leave the hubbub of the

encampment and the bustle of the traders' stalls and slip into the sanctuary, with its groves of olive trees, its statues and its shrines; its temples with their colonnades lit by dancing flames from braziers and torches, orange firelight in the pallor of the still-

16. *The violent struggle between the centaurs and the Lapiths, a subject chosen to adorn not only the Temple of Zeus at Olympia but the Parthenon at Athens. Marble, Athens, 447–432 BC. Height 99 cm.*

growing moon. No doubt many would converge on the Temple of Zeus to see Pheidias' great statue (see p. 16f.). But even from the outside, the building offered much to be admired. Built, as it had been, from the spoils of war (see p. 18), there were victory statues everywhere. One, gilded, glowing in the moonlight, stood at the apex of the temple's pediment, while at its feet a gold shield hung, a dedication from the Spartans for a victory in war.

Here, on the eastern pediment itself, above the great bronze doors, another victory was commemorated: the victory of Pelops over Oinomaos in the chariot race, one of the legendary origins of the Olympic Games themselves (see p. 73f.). Framed by the gods of the two rivers of Olympia, Alpheios and Kladeos, the richly painted sculptures showed the two contestants with their horses and supporters readying themselves before the race, while in the centre, Zeus himself looked on. Go to the western side, and you could see depicted there the struggle between the half-horse, half-men centaurs and the mythical peoples called the Lapiths; a struggle frozen, ended by the magisterial command, the outstretched arm of the implacable Apollo, the victory of the Olympian god of light over dark primeval chaos.

Beneath the pediments, a series of twelve self-contained sculptural blocks or metopés proclaimed the triumph of Olympia's other founding hero, Heracles, over a similar array of primordial beasts – the hydra and the birds of Stymphalos, the Arcadian boar, the Nemean lion – while others showed his feats of superhuman strength, as when he bore the very sky upon his shoulders. In some of them there was another figure beside Heracles himself. Athene in her helmet and her gorgon-headed goatskin[58] stood beside him, supporting him and offering encouragement. This was a perfect piece of studied symbolism: man struggling against the odds, against all manner of adversities, and, despite exhaustion, winning through thanks not only to his own tenacity and strength but to his partnership with the divine. For without the gods' help, nothing was possible.

By the western portico old men perhaps were reminiscing how – was it already almost thirty years before? – the historian Herodotus had mesmerized them as he read from his new *Histories*, of the great exploits of their ancestors at Marathon and Salamis, Plataea and Thermopylae, how the Greeks had united to defeat the Persians. Some may have wondered if maybe they might come across that other historian whom they had met the at the previous Olympiad (420 BC): Thucydides,[59] the exiled Athenian general, rich from his gold mines up in Thrace. His was a grimly modern history, a meticulous account of the wars which had so recently plagued Greece and which many feared would soon break out again.

17. *The 7th century BC Temple of Hera today. In 416 BC, its pediments were crowned by terracotta discs painted in black, yellow, white and red.*

But there were other wonders to be seen, not least the already ancient Temple of Zeus' consort, Hera. It had been completed perhaps two centuries before (seventh century BC), though, if you asked an Elean, he would tell you it was even older.[60] Smaller and squatter than the Temple of Zeus, it had originally been built of

wood – indeed the rafters and the infrastructure which supported
the terracotta roof-tiles were still wooden. So, too, were most of
the columns. But over time some of these columns had begun to
decay, and, rather than replace them like for like, the Olympian
authorities had decreed that they should be renewed in stone. By
416 BC the building was a curious amalgam of materials and styles
– for each new column was subtly different: in width, in style of
fluting, in the design of their capitals. It was a glorious
architectural mishmash, united only by the colours and the
patterns of its paintwork – like the patterns on the terracotta
discs fixed high up on the apex of each pediment, each decorated
with a geometric pattern in black and yellow, white and red.

Inside the temple, the cult statues were equally archaic.

18. *The Chest of Kypselos was rich in representations of mythological scenes like those depicted on this sarcophagus. Painted terracotta, Clazomenae, 600–575 BC. Length 2.3 m; width 1.1 m.*

Pausanias tells us what he saw:

> In the Temple of Hera is a statue of Zeus. The statue of Hera
> is sitting on a throne; Zeus is standing beside her. He is
> bearded and wears a helmet. Both are primitive works of art.

He goes on to list other statues, including an Athene; a Demeter;
a Persephone; statues of Apollo and Artemis facing one another; a
Fortune and a Dionysus; a winged Victory. He concludes:

19. *Wearing his lion skin and wielding his club, images of Heracles, one of the mythical founders of the Games, were found throughout Olympia. Fragment of painted pottery, Athens, 500–470 BC. Height 3.8 cm.*

> I cannot say who the sculptors were, but in my opinion these works are also very ancient … All I have mentioned are made from ivory and gold.[61]

Also inside the temple, the visitor was shown four treasured objects. The first was one of antiquity's most celebrated works of art, a cedar-wood box, elaborately carved and inlaid with ivory and gold, the so-called Chest of Kypselos. Fashioned in perhaps the seventh century BC, its sides and lid were rich in their array of mythological scenes. The Trojan War, the voyage of the Argo, Pelops and his chariot race to win Hippodameia, Theseus and Ariadne, Perseus and the Medusa, the two sons of Oedipus, Eteokles and Polyneikes, fighting to be king, the journeys of Odysseus, the labours of Heracles – all these (and more) appeared somewhere on the chest. Pausanias in his *Guide* devoted more space to it than to any other work of art.

The second object possessed a status verging upon that of a religious relic. It was the bed of Hippodameia, the maiden for whose hand Pelops had competed in the legendary chariot race, which some saw as the archetype of the Olympic Games (see p. 73f.). Pausanias' reaction to the relic was distinctly lukewarm. Kypselos' Chest must have exhausted even his enthusiasm. The bed, he said, was 'not particularly big; inlaid for the most part with ivory … the plaything, they say, of Hippodameia.'[62] Sadly, he is similarly brief about the other two items, both of which were of great importance to the Games:

> Iphitus' discus and the table on which they lay out the
> victors' crowns … Inscribed on Iphitus' discus are the
> words of the truce which the men of Elis proclaim at the
> Olympic Festivals. The inscription is not written in a
> straight line, but rather the words run round the discus
> in a circle. The table is made out of ivory and gold.[63]

Neither of these objects has survived, and the text of the truce, which Pausanias could so easily have documented, is lost to us. No other ancient source records it either, so we do not know the words which the three heralds sent from Elis broadcast, as they wound their way around the sprawling world of Greece, their

20. *The Bouleuterion today, looking from one of the apsidal halls towards the chamber which housed the terrifying statue of Zeus of Oaths (see p. 56).*

heads wreathed in the sacred olive, their sturdy staffs in hand, proclaiming as they went to the coming Games. If Pausanias was tired from his examination of the temple, so, too, we might suppose, were the sightseers. So they headed back to the visitors' encampment, whose enticements we can only imagine.

Sunrise saw a change of pace. The officials and the stewards were already up and bustling. The judges strutted in their purple robes.

The Bouleuterion (council chamber) was swept and clean. Soon the whole Altis was abuzz, for this was the morning when it all began.

We do not know exactly what happened in those early hours. It has been well conjectured that a purifying ritual was performed, similar perhaps to that which the *Hellanodikai* had undergone two days before at the Fountain of Piera (see p. 45). A proclamation is imagined, too, in which those who were barred from taking any part in the forthcoming Festival were ordered to withdraw. These were not only married women, but any man with hands (or conscience) stained by blood-guilt or by sacrilege. Such purifications and proclamations were common at the beginning of Greek festivals, and the fact that there is no recorded evidence may simply mean that no one thought them remarkable enough to record.

We know what happened next, however – and, again, it is mainly thanks to Pausanias. The setting was just outside the Altis to the south: the Bouleuterion, a great complex of two apsidal buildings,[64] flanking on each side a central chamber, all linked by a long and elegantly colonnaded frontage. This was where the Olympic Council held its meetings. Here too they kept their archives. Presiding over all of their proceedings was an awe-inspiring statue of Zeus. Pausanias described it:

> The statue of Zeus in the Bouleuterion is of all his statues the one most likely to strike terror into the hearts of wrongdoers. Its epithet is 'God of Oaths' and in each hand it holds a thunderbolt. It is the tradition that, standing before this statue, the athletes, their fathers and their brothers – yes, even their trainers – should swear over a dismembered boar an oath to do no wrong against the Olympic Games. The athletes themselves make a further oath that they have strictly followed the full regulations of training for ten successive months. Another oath is made by those who determine whether athletes can compete in the boys' category ... that they will make their judgement honestly and without taking bribes, and that they will keep whatever they learn about the contestant confidential, whether they admit him to the Games or not ... In front of the feet of the God of Oaths is a small bronze panel on which are inscribed

21. *Shame set in stone: 'Footprints' on their bases are now all that remain of the bronze 'zanes' statues of Zeus set up from fines imposed on cheating athletes.*

some verses designed to strike fear into those who break their oath.[65]

Even by 416 BC that oath had never knowingly been broken. In over three and a half centuries no athlete had ever been accused of cheating. But in the next generation, that would all change. Seven Olympiads later, in 388 BC, the Festival was rocked by scandal when a boxer, Eupolus of Thessaly, was found to have bribed his three opponents. Outraged, the *Hellanodikai* fined all four men, and with the money they erected six bronze statues of Zeus, which they placed on a platform opposite the treasuries (fig. 11). Inscribed on them were the names of the offenders, together with admonitory verses. Among them was one reminding athletes that they should win not with money, but through the speed of their feet or the strength of their physique. It was a warning which not everyone would heed. Over the years, these six would be joined by at least ten other *Zanes,* as the statues set up from the fines of cheating athletes were called. Their bases can still be seen today (fig. 21).

The great oath had been sworn. Chastened perhaps by the power of Zeus of Oaths, and profoundly aware of the possibilities for stratospheric glory or for abject shame, the athletes and their entourages emerged into the sunlight and the crowds. All eyes were on the boys, many of them accompanied by older lovers offering advice and words of last minute encouragement. For these boys were the heroes of this first day of the Games and it was time for them to compete.[66]

So much to do with the Olympic Festival has been obscured by

*22. One of the Hellanodikai sits in judgement, his pose perhaps deliberately mirroring that of Pheidias' statue of Zeus. Red-figure pottery, Athens, 450–430 BC. Height 26 cm.*

time, not least the sequence of many of the events. We do not know which of the three contests came first, the running, wrestling or boxing, though, as this is the order in which we first hear of them, it was perhaps the sequence in which they took place. The boys' foot-race and wrestling had both been introduced into the schedule of the Games over two hundred years earlier, in 632 BC; four Olympiads later (616 BC) they had been joined by the boys' boxing. Between these two dates, the Olympic officials had also experimented with introducing another contest, the boys' pentathlon. It made its appearance for one Festival only, in 628 BC, before being quietly dropped.

Now the crowds were lining the stadium for the first event. Some of the older men gathered on the south embankment could perhaps just remember how the race track had been dug out maybe forty years before: how it had been deepened and flattened, how the old trophies, shields and armour, which had lined the course, had been grubbed up and, with old-fashioned sculptures, had been thrown onto the hill, and the excavated earth piled up on top of them,[67] the whole construction supported by a retaining wall of stone, some four metres high.[68] To the north, still more spectators took their places on the Platform of the Treasuries, while more thronged where the Hill of Kronos began its steep and wooded rise above the plain.[69]

Across at the eastern end, the young athletes, oiled and naked, were limbering up, their trainers anxiously beside them, advising and encouraging, reminding them of all that they had learned. Two hundred metres away, their goal, the finish – a line of stone

23. 'A naked man can run more quickly than a clothed one': oiled, naked and sprinkled with glistening dust, a sprinter races to victory. Painted pottery, Miletus, 530–500 BC. Height 34 cm.

sunk in the sand; and standing by it, in their purple robes, the *Hellanodikai*, alert and ready for the crucial judgement as the boys sped by. Of course, there were years when there was a clear and certain winner. People still spoke of young Polymnestor, swift as the wind, who had passed into legend almost two centuries before. Back home in Miletus, by the turquoise sea, he had been tending his goats one day when a startled hare had shot up at his feet and bounded off across the scrubby hills, sweet with the scent of marjoram. In an instant, Polymnestor was in pursuit, darting after it, always gaining on it, capturing it in his hands.[70] At Olympia there had been no one who could match him. But he was rare. It was unlikely that another such would be competing this year.

Now the boys were ranged along the starting line.[71] The heats were all behind them. This was the final race, the only race which mattered. The blood pounding in their brains, they set their sights down the long tunnel of spectators to the great eastern pediment of the Temple of Zeus beyond. This was their inspiration. For them to win, Zeus himself must grant them speed.

All athletes, men and boys (though not the charioteers), competed naked. Legend told how the tradition had begun three centuries before, when one, Orsippos, had lost his loincloth as he competed in a race which he had then gone on to win. Many put this win down to his nakedness. In fact, Pausanias (with an uncharacteristic lack of charity) writes: 'My view is that he intentionally let his loincloth fall off, because he knew that a naked man can run more quickly than a clothed one.'[72]

To protect them from the sun, as well as to enhance their performance, the athletes applied olive oil to their naked torsos, then covered themselves with dust. For contact sports like wrestling, the dust had the effect of making it easier to get a hold on the opponent's body, but there were other reasons for their powdering themselves. In later years the use of the correct dust for the correct purposes became quite a science:

> The dust of clay is good for disinfecting and for giving balance to excessive sweaters; dust from terracotta is good for opening closed pores for perspiration; dust from asphalt is good for heating the chilled; black and yellow earth are both good for softening and for maintaining. Yellow dust also adds glisten and is a delight to see on a nice body which is in good shape. The dust should be sprinkled with a fluid motion of the wrist and with fingers spread apart and the dust more like drizzle than a thunderburst so that it covers the athlete like soft down. [73]

So now the boys stood, naked, glistening and waiting. The trainers had withdrawn. The judges were primed. Adrenalin was rushing in their ears. And then, behind them, the trumpet brayed. And they were off, their bare feet pummelling the earthen track, their chests out, elbows jabbing, muscles rippling, hands flexed, carving the warm air, heedless of the throaty roar which rose on either side, and carried them, a thundering wave of sound to speed them on, on, forward, till it cast them all across the finishing line and their legs could not support them, shaking, feeble now, their lungs on fire and fighting for their breath. But for one of them, and only one, a sense of exultation such as he had never known before. He was the victor. He had won. At home, his name would be immortal. Here at Olympia, a statue would forever tell men who he was. [74] The 91st Games had produced their first champion.

As his trainer, parents and lover joined with the men from his home city in congratulating the young sprinter – and as his unsuccessful rivals, each with his head hung low, tried to ignore the cat-calls and the insults heaped upon them – the judges' minds were already focused on the next event: the wrestling. Already, as the lots had fallen out, the boys were lined up in their pairs, not svelte and agile like the runners, but, to the eyes of many, muscle-bound and brutish. It had been long debated, and would be for centuries to come, whether it was a kindness to bring boys to such a peak of strength at such an early age.[75] Very few of them would go on to compete successfully as men; most burned out by adulthood; and even among men, the pressure of fighting in the ring could lead to mental imbalance, the consequence of which at times could be spectacularly chilling (see p. 144f.).

---

24. *A wrestler brings down his opponent using a grip called the 'flying mare'. Red-figure pottery, Athens, c.430 BC. Height 8.3 cm.*

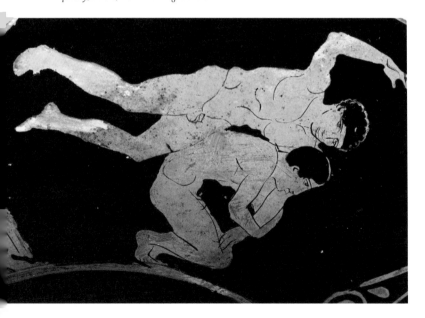

As with the adult version of the sport, the wrestler engaged at
all times from an upright stance, pushing, shoving, trying to
unbalance his opponent, struggling to get him on the ground –
for, bring down your antagonist three times, and you had won. It
was a mix of upper body strength and nimble footwork; size in
itself was not everything. One famous wrestler, perhaps the most
renowned of all, had learned this a century before. Milo, from the
south Italian city, Croton, was one of those rare athletes who had
won the wrestling contest as a boy and then gone on to carry off
a string of victories in manhood. As an adult he won five times
over twenty years, in five successive Olympiads. In his sixth, he
was beaten – not because he had weakened, but because, as
Pausanias records, 'he could not defeat his fellow citizen,
Timasitheos, a young man, who refused to come to close quarters
with him.[76] Milo was a veritable legend.'

> They say, too, that Milo carried his own statue into the Altis
> … He would clasp a pomegranate in his hand so firmly that
> no one could prize it from him by force – yet the pressure of
> his hold did not damage it … He would tie a cord around
> his head as if it were a victory ribbon or a crown; then he
> would hold his breath and filling the veins in his head with
> blood he would snap the cord simply through the strength
> of his veins.[77]

Even the manner of his death was quite remarkable. The story
is that he was killed by wild animals. It goes like this: in the land
of Croton he happened to find a tree-trunk which was being dried
out; wedges had been hammered into it to keep it open; now
Milo, self-confident as ever, thrust his hands into the trunk
[meaning to split it], but the wedges slipped, and Milo was

trapped, and the wolves, which roam the land of Croton in great packs, tore him apart.[78]

It was, of course, in the boys' wrestling and boxing in particular, that the importance of the *Hellanodikai*'s decision with regard to age and fitness to compete was crucial. Many years before, in 588 BC, when Milo's compatriot Glycon had won the men's foot-race, one youth, Pythagoras from the mountainous Aegean island of Samos, had been disqualified from taking part in the boys' boxing and mocked for being effeminate. Just why this should have been is hard to tell – he went on to take part in the men's competition and defeated all comers.[79]

Naked, liberally doused with olive oil and caked with sand (see p. 63), the wrestlers resembled nothing so much as the mud-men of mythology, risen from the earth at the sowing of the dragon's teeth. Their contest must have appeared equally primeval, as they circled one another, each looking for a hold, watching for the opportunity to trip up his opponent; preening, strutting, drinking in the adulation of the audience when it was done; each young man nursing an ambition to be better even than Milo but none destined to achieve his dream. This year, it was the turn of Nikostratos to be the last boy standing. He had journeyed to Olympia from Heraia, a village in the mountains of Arcadia, where Pan, god of the wild, was worshipped in a rustic shrine.[80] For him, the feasting and festivities would go on long into the night both on this day and when he returned home.

The wrestling done, a fresh troop of muscle-bound young men appeared before the crowd, the faces of many bearing the marks of their chosen discipline: fractured noses, deformed ears, split and ill-healed cheekbones. Already the boy-boxers carried their scars with pride. Indeed, many of the older men considered them particularly attractive. Even Pheidias, it will be recalled, that doyen of all things beautiful, had conducted an affair with Pantarkes of Elis, the young boxing champion (see p. 27).

Like the wrestling, the boxing probably took place in the sacred Altis, some distance in front of the Temple of Zeus, on an area of flattened earth, raked smooth and sandy and cordoned off from the spectators by a low picket fence.[81] Its proximity to the temple and the other shrines served to emphasize the ancient religious connotations of these contact sports far removed from a mere trial of strength for its own sake. Rather, it was a contest to see whose strength was the more pleasing to the god. The more blood was shed and damage caused in the process, and the harder the outcome was to reach, the more honour was paid to the god. It could be a messy, painful business. One later adult boxer, Androleus, wrote an epigram to celebrate his career in three different Greek Games. It read: 'I left one of my ears at Olympia and one of my eyes at Plataea. At Delphi they took me for dead and carried me out.'[82]

While many of the boys would not possess the sheer brute force of older practitioners, some would, and some undoubtedly made up in enthusiasm for what they lacked in technique. Yet there were no classifications of boxers by weight or age, so, in theory at least, a precocious yet still not fully-grown 15-year-old could face a huge and strapping adversary almost five years his senior (and with five years more experience to boot).

As in the wrestling, pairs of boxers were drawn by lot, with winners in the first round going through to the next until the last two standing met. Whether these initial rounds took place simultaneously or whether consecutively, we do not know, but undoubtedly it could all take some time – the growing excitement of the crowd drowning out the dull crack of leather on jaw and the grunts and groans of the contestants (for more on the boxing competition, see p. 139f.). Passions among the onlookers reached breaking point, especially among those who had a special interest in one of the boxers.

Several Olympiads later, this proved to be almost the undoing of one member of a young boxer's entourage. Pisodoros of Rhodes came from a long line of champion boxers. His maternal grandfather, his uncles and his brother had all won many prizes. But in the months before the Olympic Games, tragedy struck. His father, who had been coaching him, died unexpectedly. It was hard to find a personal instructor who knew his ways as his father had. Until, that is, a mysterious new coach stepped in. Pisodoros blossomed. He entered the Olympics and progressed to the final bout. When he landed the winning blow and his opponent fell flailing to his knees, the crowd erupted in a welter of excitement. His coach (like everybody then, a stranger to underwear) leapt over the fence, robes hitched high to avoid being caught. And this was the moment of truth. For the watching spectators it was all too clear: the coach was a woman! Pisodoros had been trained by his own mother, Pherenike (whose name, appropriately enough, meant 'Bringer of Victory'). But women were barred from the Olympic Games on pain of death. Pausanias even saw the place of execution for those who broke the rule:

> On the road to Olympia from Skillos, just before you cross the Alpheios, is a mountain with high sheer cliffs. Its name is Trypaion. The law of Elis is that from this cliff should be thrown any woman discovered at the Olympic Festival, or even on the other side of the Alpheios, on prohibited days.

---

25. *Their hands and wrists bound with leather thongs, two boxers slug it out. One appears to have suffered a facial injury. Red-figure pottery, Athens, 490–480 BC. Height 31.2 cm.*

Actually, they say that no woman ever has been caught,
except only Pherenike ...[83]

The *Hellanodikai* were outraged. A court of judgement was
convened. But rather than adhere strictly to the letter of the law,
they let Pherenike off. She was from such an illustrious sporting
family, it seemed unjust to kill her. Indeed, from that day she was
known by a new name: Kallipateira ('Mrs Goodfather').
However, they did impose a new rule on Olympic trainers.
Henceforth they too, like the athletes, would have to appear
naked at the Games – just to be certain.

In 416 BC, though, all this was in the future, and now at last the
(still-clothed) trainer of the triumphant boy boxer could leap the
fence and hug his protégé to him in fervent congratulation. The
champion tied the victor's ribbon round his head, and clutched
the palm branch in his aching hands, his brain still dizzy from the
many blows that had rained on him so heavily that hot dry August
afternoon, while his opponents, battered and broken, limped off,
leaning hard on their supporters' arms.

The boys' events were done. The first day's trials were over. The
crowds dispersed, debating everything that they had seen that day,
some no doubt disputing a decision of the judges; others
discussing how to spend the coming night; many anticipating the
excitement of the morning. For today there were no more official
events. But in the morning would take place one of the most
intoxicating spectacles of all: the chariot race. And word had it
that for the first time in Olympia's long history, one man was
entering no less than seven chariots. With rumours rippling
through the crowds, the speculation grew and stories were
exchanged about that one man, Alcibiades, whose tent stood
proudly on the plain, whose day would come tomorrow.

# CHAPTER 3

# FUNERAL GAMES

## DAY 2 (FULL MOON MINUS ONE)

Now that the sun had set and moonrise had heralded a new day, the atmosphere was more relaxed. On this, the full moon's eve, there were no official ceremonies, no commitments to prevent the delegates and the spectators from drawing breath or strolling round the sacred precinct, taking in the sights.

For many who had not taken the chance to investigate it the day before, one of the main attractions of the evening would have been the celebrated tent of Alcibiades (see p. 39), its access closely guarded by a hand-picked retinue of youths. Undoubtedly for every man who looked at it in wonder, there would have been another who viewed it with suspicion: its Eastern luxury, its ostentation, its curiously un-Greek presence on the plain. Yet, for Alcibiades, opinions like these were immaterial. He was already on record as remarking that to be spoken of at all was all that mattered; there was no such thing as bad publicity.[84]

No doubt those idle sightseers observed a flurry of activity around the tent. Any private banquet Alcibiades might be hosting would be attended by the richest and most powerful men from Athens' allied states – perhaps, too, by some with whom she may have been in conflict. This (and other even more exclusive meetings) was the ideal opportunity to lobby Athens' rising star: for leading citizens of great commercial hubs like Ephesus, Miletus and Cyrene to solicit his support; for statesmen anxious about Athens' military policy to press for their withdrawal from

Melos (see p. 37). With every new encounter, Alcibiades' kudos grew. As the athletes and spectators settled down to sleep it must have been with a degree of satisfaction that he contemplated how, with luck, next morning, there would not be one man in all the tens of thousands in this tented town who would not be speaking of him, or how in but a few days time he would have the multitude quite literally eating from his hand.

On that next morning, as the rising sun infused the eastern sky, its rays fell first upon the Hill of Kronos with its thickly wooded slopes, and minutes later, in the sanctuary, the sculptures on the apex of the temple roofs. As the light spread downwards and across the columns, picking out the statues and the trees, the altars and the sacred grove, it brought into sharp focus the low walls which enclosed the mound of Pelops, itself surrounded by white poplar trees. Located between the temples of the two great gods, Zeus and Hera, the Pelopion, as it was called, was one of the

26. *Model chariot wheels dedicated after a victory in a race. Bronze, Argos, sixth century BC. Diameter 10.2 cm.*

most sacred sites at Olympia. Whether physically or spiritually, it was to form the focus of all of the activities performed on this, the second full day of the Games, for it was, in part, to Pelops that the Games owed their very origin.

Even in 416 BC, the story of Pelops was an ancient one. Dark legends told how, as a boy, he had been butchered by his father, Tantalos, cut into tiny pieces and boiled up in a stew, and fed to the gods in an unholy offering. Only the goddess Demeter tasted the strange meat. The others knew the truth immediately. They punished Tantalos, and with great ritual and care they reassembled Pelops' body, fitted him with an ivory shoulder (to replace that eaten by Demeter) and breathed life back into him.

But it was for his accomplishments in adulthood that he would be specifically remembered. As a young man, he left his native Anatolia (in modern Turkey) and came to Greece. Here, in Pisa (map, p. 224) King Oinomaos had received a prophecy that whoever married his daughter, Hippodameia, would kill him. So the king challenged all his daughter's suitors to a chariot race. Whoever defeated him could marry her. Whoever failed would die. By the time Pelops reached Pisa, the heads of thirteen suitors grinned lifelessly from wooden stakes in Oinomaos' palace.

Pelops himself decided to take no chances. With his feisty team of winged horses, a gift from the gods, he should easily have won. But to ensure his victory, he resorted to cunning. With extravagant bribes, he persuaded Myrtilos, Oinomaos' charioteer, to replace the bronze lynchpins, which fixed the wheels onto the axle, with lynchpins made from beeswax. And so it was that, in the race which followed, as Oinomaos' wheels rotated ever faster, the friction caused the wax to melt, the chariot disintegrated and the dying king was dragged behind his bolting horses. Pelops had won. He claimed Hippodameia as his bride but rather than rewarding Myrtilos for helping him, he threw him off a cliff into the sea.

To us, Pelops' behaviour is patently unsporting, and undeserving of heroic celebration. Surprising as it may seem, however, the Greeks not only venerated Pelops as a hero, but, according to some ancient sources, inaugurated funeral games (athletic contests held in honour of the recently deceased) in his memory, which in turn grew into the Olympic Games. His bones themselves were kept at Pisa, in a bronze chest in a mausoleum near the Sanctuary of Artemis, itself close by the grave-mound of Hippodameia's thirteen suitors who had fought fair and lost.[85] At Olympia, his image was everywhere. In the Temple of Hera, the fabulous cedar-wood chest of Kypselos, carved and adorned with figures made of ivory and gold, showed not only Pelops and his horses at full gallop, but his funeral games, too, presided over by the hero Heracles.[86] And on the eastern pediment of the Temple of Zeus – the rising sun reflected on the metal reins, the paintwork rich and vivid – a marble Pelops prepared to mount his marble chariot.

All of the contests on this second day of the Olympic Festival were given over to commemorating Pelops: the races with horses and chariots in which Pelops had himself competed; the events of the pentathlon, themselves a recreation of the founding funeral games. All were, in their way, a preparation for the solemn celebration of the rituals of death which soon would be performed beneath the full moon at the hero's sacred shrine.

Now, with the dawn, the tented city by the banks of the rivers

27. *Winged victory hovers over Pelops, the hero of Olympia, while he gazes longingly at Hippodameia (bottom left) and Myrtilos, his opponent's charioteer (bottom right), tampers with a wheel. Red-figure pottery, Puglia, southern Italy, 350–340 BC. Height 58.4 cm.*

Alpheios and Kladeos had sprung to life. In the early heat, men were already breakfasting, most dipping chunks of unleavened bread – bought from the vendors' stalls, baked through the night on fires – into cups of watered wine, accompanied perhaps by a handful of black olives and a few figs. From elsewhere, the smell of roasting meat drifted across the encampment. For over a hundred years, since the time of the great wrestler Milo, athletes had begun to understand the importance of a high protein diet, turning away from their previous 'dry fare' of cheese, dried figs and bread.[87] Milo himself was said (somewhat implausibly) to have enjoyed a daily consumption of twenty pounds of meat and twenty pounds of bread, all washed down with two gallons of wine.[88] Moreover, for some seven Olympiads now, athletes had been increasingly following the example of the pentathlete, Ikkos of Tarentum, and submitting themselves to a diet as rigorous as their physical training.[89]

*28. Votive statuettes of horses such as these were common at Olympia from the early period of the Games. Bronze, Olympia, c. 800–700 BC. Height 9 cm.*

For such pentathletes, their great test was to come this afternoon. Perhaps they spent the morning training. If they did, they would have had the gymnasium and the palaestra to themselves. For, even now the crowds were streaming from their tents and round the side of the sacred enclosure to the great hippodrome which stretched out for a quarter of a mile towards the east, twice the length of the athletic stadium.[90]

Few at these Games, if any, could remember how, in the years before the building of the Temple of Zeus,[91] the races had been run across the plain, the riders and the charioteers whipping on their horses to the finish by the sanctuary of Pelops. Now, with the Altis becoming increasingly crowded, an area of flat land, dedicated to horse racing, had been laid out to the east: the hippodrome. The races still began and finished at the western end, nearest the Pelopion; perhaps by a newly-planted grove of olive trees, grown from cuttings taken from those which Heracles was said to have planted round the original finishing post.[92]

By now, the first of the spectators had arrived, many taking their places on the northern side, where the ground sloped gently up to a low ridge, affording the best view of the final furlong. Opposite them, on the south, still more were gathering on the artificial mound between the racecourse and the River Alpheios. This was the side the horses would pass first, as they galloped for their anticlockwise turn at the far, eastern end – a moment of potential danger and excitement, which was why so many more spectators were already there.

In a short time, all was ready for the first event. As the tens of thousands of spectators strained to see, their expectation almost palpable, the racehorses were led in by their grooms,[93] their jockeys – many of them slave boys bought from Africa[94] – looking small and vulnerable on the glistening sleek backs of their horses.

Skilled in the use of reins and spurs and curb-less bits and bridles, they did not yet know of saddles or of stirrups, so the boys rode bareback, crouching high up near the horses' necks.

These jockeys, like the grooms, were the elite of slaves, and the horses that they cared for were among the most expensive and high-status items of their day. In much of Greece, where for a peasant even to eke out a modest harvest was back-breaking work, the thin soil meant that growing enough fodder for a horse was beyond the means of most. Even in democratic Athens there was a strict class system, in which to own a horse was to be a member of the aristocracy. Moreover, in the iconography of art, horses were often associated not with mere men, but with heroes, that specific band of mortals who, through great deeds, were worshipped after death as if they were near-gods.[95]

If owning a horse was a sign of wealth, owning a thoroughbred racehorse – one that could compete in the Olympic Games – was a sign that one belonged to the political elite. To breed or buy or stable such a racehorse was to be a member of an exclusive club of fabulously rich kings and aristocrats. It was a passion which in many ways transcended the mundane politics of daily life and linked the most powerful men and families across the breadth of the Mediterranean Sea, from Sicily to Sardis.

It may be that one such aristocrat from Athens, Gryllus, was at these Games with his sixteen-year-old son, Xenophon. In later years, Xenophon, now a seasoned general, would own an estate near Olympia and write an influential book, *On Horsemanship,* in which he detailed what to look for in a horse, and how to stable it; how best to mount it and to ride it; how best to train a

29. *His whip raised in his right hand, a bareback jockey urges his horse on ever faster.*
*Red-figure pottery, Athens, 450–430 BC. Height 34.3 cm.*

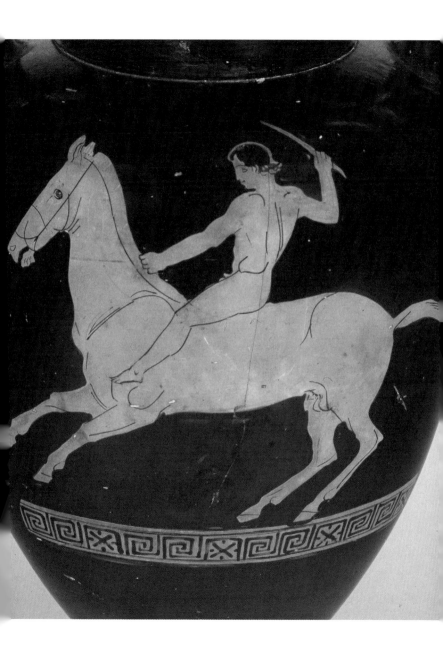

30. *A judge helps a struggling boy jockey onto his mount. Red-figure pottery, Athens, 440–420 BC. Height 33 cm.*

racehorse. His advice is followed to this day.

After the racehorses and riders had paraded round the hippodrome, it was the turn of the chariots. Discussions were perhaps already underway which, eight years later, would allow for two-horse chariots to compete in the Olympics, but for now there was one race alone: for four-horse chariots. Lightweight and low, these chariots were built for speed, not safety. The horses, rigorously trained and fed on the best fodder possible, were used to working as a team. Racing four abreast, the central pair was harnessed by a yoke joined to the chariot's pole, while the two on the outside ran as trace-horses, trained for the critical tight turns, responsive to their driver's reins.

As they entered the hippodrome at Olympia, the horses, many of which had already raced at games at Delphi or Nemea or the Isthmus, picked up the excitement of the crowd, even as, reined in, they slowly walked the course, rounding the far turn sedately, knowing that it was here the greatest danger lay.

Now that the great procession of chariots and horses, some already snorting and whinnying with anticipation, had completed its procession around the hippodrome, it became clear to every one of the spectators packed shoulder-to-shoulder on the dusty rise – some standing high on tiptoe, others jostling their neighbours for a better view – that the rumours had been true. For the first time in Olympic history, one man was entering a record seven chariots. Even if they had not recognized his colours, they would have known him. His wealth, his showmanship and his audacity were legendary. He was already the darling of these Games, and there he was, in his rich tunic, taking his place in the owners' enclosure by the judges' seats next to the finishing line: Alcibiades.

This year, there may have been a second cause for wonder. For it was around this time that the new holding pens were introduced. Built by Kleoetas, son of Aristokles, originally from Kydonia (modern Chania) in Crete, the so-called *Hippaphesis* was a V-shaped structure in which the chariots and horses were staggered behind gates. At the turn of a lever, a bronze eagle (the bird of Zeus) would rise high above the altar at the apex, while a dolphin (the symbol of Apollo) similarly bronze, descended to the earth.[96] At this, the gates would be mechanically opened; first those at the back, farthest from the apex, then the rest in order, to allow the competitors to take up their position at the starting line. It was pure theatre – a choreography of chariots and horses to delight the crowd.

But for now, the chariots had left the hippodrome. The grooms

31. **Previous spread:** *In art, horses were associated not only with wealth but with heroic prowess, as in the mysterious procession depicted on the Parthenon Frieze. Marble, Athens, 438–432 BC. Height 99 cm.*

and riders had manoeuvred the horses into the *Hippaphesis* – with difficulty, no doubt, as the contraption was so new and unfamiliar. The eagle rose. The dolphin dropped. The trumpet rang out loud and clear. The horse race had begun. Just one lap, that was all – a race of half a mile. Given their heads, the horses needed no encouragement. The jockeys nonetheless hunched low, their faces near their horses' ears, shouting their encouragement as they lashed their whips against their horses' flanks. A shuddering of hooves on the hard earth; a haze of dust; and then the turn – the horses bunched together, dangerously close. Jockeys unseated, fallen on the earth, curled up, trying ineffectively to guard their tiny bodies from the pounding, pummelling hooves. Then, as the trumpet brayed again, the final furlong's headlong dash. The winning jockey's exultation. The owner's pride; his knowledge that his standing in the world had just shot higher.

Even a riderless horse could win the race, as had once happened a century before, when, in a race for mares (since discontinued), a horse called Aura (Breeze), owned by a Corinthian, Pheidolas, had thrown her jockey early on.

32. *Standing on his fragile chariot, the charioteer urges on his horses. Black-figure pottery, Athens, 410–400 BC. Height 6.75 cm. Donated by George Dennis.*

Nevertheless, she kept on running well – she turned the post and, when she heard the trumpet, lengthened her stride and passed the Hellanodikai in first place. Then, when she realized that she had won, she stopped. The men of Elis declared Pheidolas

the winner and allowed him to set up a statue of his mare.[97]

The thrill of the horse race was extraordinary, but it was, if anything, a mere prelude to the chief event of the morning: the chariot race. Again the four-horse chariots trundled into the hippodrome, but now they took their places in the *Hippaphesis*. As the pairs of gates were opened, their drivers, keeping their reins tight, steered their horses at a walk to the starting line: first the outside pair of chariots, and then the next, and then the next again, until they all were in position.

Already, the charioteers had slid their feet tight into the foot-straps which would let them lean back at the crucial moment for the turn. The leather reins were in their hands. Each man of them could feel the heat rise from his horses' rumps as he stood tall, waiting, perhaps praying, making a private vow to his patron god. For each knew that, while their chariots were technologically perfect in their design for speed, they would offer no protection in a crash. Perhaps there were a few who remembered the vivid description in a tragedy produced on stage in Athens twelve years before, when Euripides described Hippolytus' team of horses bolting from a mysterious bull which chased them on the beach:

> The wheel-rim caught against a rock, and it buckled,
> throwing him to the ground. It was all confusion. Hubs of
> wheels and lynchpins spiralled through the air, while he
> himself, the poor man, was dragged along the ground,
> caught in the entanglement of reins which he could not
> escape from, cracking his head against the rocks, ripping
> off his flesh … [98]

33. *The speed and danger of the race: a charioteer crouches low as a rival team of horses presses him hard on his left. Black-figure pottery, Athens, 500–480 BC. Height 10.2 cm.*

Perhaps they remembered, too, the fate of King Oinomaos in the chariot race with Pelops, whose statue glinted in the sun before them on the central barrier. Here was another hurdle they must overcome: the morning sun hanging, blazing in the east, blinding both charioteers and horses.

But for now their focus was all on the race. As the tension in the crowd rose almost to breaking point, the trumpet blared out. They were off! The thundering of hooves on the hard dry ground; the cries of charioteers to horses; the deafening roar of the spectators – here was the pure adrenalin of the Olympics. And now already, after two stades,[99] the teams had reached the altar, the *Taraxippos*, the cenotaph to Pelops' charioteer Myrtilos,[100] where it was said the horses could be often spooked, and they were making their first turn. To a man, each charioteer reined in his inner trace-horse,[101] letting the horses on the outside gallop faster, as the charioteers themselves leant out from the turn. This was the danger time, the time when accidents were virtually inevitable: split-second judgements wrongly made; distances miscalculated by a fatal inch; a wheel caught; a chariot crashed; a confusion of horses tangled terrified in reins; drivers desperately trying to extricate themselves before the team behind crashed headlong into them.

Meanwhile, those teams still in the race were thundering towards the next turn, as

stewards and officials battled desperately to clear the track behind
them. Six laps they had to race – the field becoming more sparse
with each turn – until at last those which remained, through luck
or skill, swung into the home strait.

34. *The bull rises from the sea to terrify Hippolytus' horses, a scene (directly inspired by
Euripides' play) familiar to the spectators of 416 BC. Red-figure pottery, Puglia,
c. 340–320 BC. Height 106.7 cm. Bequeathed by Sir William Temple.*

Again, as in the horse race earlier, when the first chariot rounded the final bend, the trumpet began to bray, its harsh notes joining with the roar of the spectators in one last deafening crescendo. The leading chariot, so flimsy to look at, so low to the ground; its four-spoked wheels a blur of movement; its charioteer crouched low, flicking at his four foam-speckled horses with his goad as they pounded the earth hard with their galloping hooves – now, the leading chariot had reached the finish. The result was clear. The winning owner: Alcibiades.

Closely behind: the second chariot. Again, its owner: Alcibiades. And then the third: like the first two, from the stable of Alcibiades.[102] Never before, and never again in the history of the Olympic Games would one man achieve such a result. Back in Athens, a victory ode would be composed, some say by Euripides, praising Alcibiades:

> But my song to you,
> Son of Clinias, is due.
> Victory is noble; how much more
> To do as never Greek before;
> To obtain in the great chariot race
> The first, the second, and third place;
> With easy step advanced to fame
> To bid the herald three times claim
> The olive for one victor's name.[103]

And as if this were not enough, Alcibiades would set up a painting on the Acropolis itself, commissioned from Aglaophon of Thasos, showing the goddess Olympia – the personification of the sacred site – placing a crown of victory on his head.[104]

At Olympia, however, in the immediate aftermath of the race, opinions were less clear-cut. Almost immediately the race was over, the circumstances of its result were to be mired in controversy:

> It is alleged that an Athenian, Diomedes, a man of high repute and a friend of Alcibiades, desperate to win a victory at Olympia, had found out about a racing chariot owned by the city of Argos. He was well aware that Alcibiades had many friends and great influence in Argos, so he got him to buy the chariot on his behalf – whereupon Alcibiades entered the chariot as his own and told Diomedes to 'get lost'. Diomedes was furious and called on the gods and men to witness how he had been treated. They say a case was brought at law …[105]

To win his famous victory, it was alleged that Alcibiades had abused his influence, power and money in a most outrageous way – even if it is true, as he possibly claimed, that he had done so in order to enhance the prestige of Athens.[106] Indeed, setting aside the cost of the chariots themselves, the value of the horses alone was stupendous: eight talents, enough and more to pay the wages of the 200-strong crew of a warship for an entire sailing season.[107]

Alcibiades' brazen display of wealth on this August day of 416 BC undoubtedly divided the spectators. Some, like his supporters from Athens and Argos, or the aristocrats of Chios, who had donated fodder for his horses, were no doubt delighted. Others shook their heads in disgust.

Among them may have been Agesilaus, the 28-year-old brother of the Spartan King Agis II. Unusually for a Spartan, Agesilaus was physically weak. Despite being lame from birth, he had been spared from infanticide, the fate of most less-than-perfect Spartan babies, and had accrued to himself a reputation not only for

bravery in the face of danger but for intelligence and kindliness.
Now, and in the period which followed, he would have cause
enough to hold Alcibiades in suspicion, if not contempt[108] – and
this shameless show of wealth served only to fuel that contempt
all the more. If money could buy victory, where was the glory?

Twenty years later, at the Olympic Games of 396 BC, Agesilaus
made his point with crushing effect:

> Seeing that people thought highly of themselves and were
> greatly esteemed because they bred racing horses, he
> persuaded his sister Kynisca to enter a chariot in the
> Olympic Games, because he wished to show the Greeks
> that being victorious there was not a sign of any great
> excellence, but simply of wealth and extravagant outlay.[109]

Kynisca, who, being a woman could not attend the Games in
person, thus became the first female victor at Olympia, where she
erected a statue with an inscription which read:

> My fathers and brothers were Spartan kings
> I proclaim myself the only woman in the whole of Greece
> to have so won the crown.
> Apelleas, the son of Kallikles, was the sculptor.[110]

Kynisca went on to win the chariot race at the next Festival, too.

For now, though, as they slowly filed out of the area of the
hippodrome and sought out lunch – some in their own tents,
others heading for the fast-food stalls which fringed the sacred
enclosure – most of the crowds had other things on their minds:
they were anticipating the pentathlon.

The pentathlon itself may well have had its origins in funeral games. In Homer's *Iliad,* the poem which more than any crystallized what it was to be Greek, much of the 23rd book is given over to a description of the games held by Achilles in honour of his fallen comrade Patroclos. In them, as on this second day of the Olympics, the first event had been a chariot race. This had been followed by a series of contests: boxing, wrestling, running, a duel between two champions until first blood was drawn, discus-throwing, archery and spear-throwing.

At the Olympic pentathlon there were five events. Gone were the archery, the boxing and the duel; in had come the long jump. And the order of the five events had changed: first discus-throwing, then the jump, then throwing the javelin, the foot-race and finally the wrestling. Unlike at Patroclos' funeral games, where the competitors for each contest were different, here it was the aim of every competing athlete to complete all five events and to emerge the overall winner. But to win, one man had to have secured victory in three events.

The exact arrangements are uncertain and the subject of fierce debate. If three of the competing athletes had each come first in the discus, the long jump or the javelin, did only they have the opportunity to take part in the last two contests – the foot-race and the wrestling – as this was the only way in which one man could achieve three clear wins? And if the same man won the first three contests, was he automatically winner of the pentathlon?

With lunch over, and the spectators crowded on the slopes surrounding the stadium, the pentathletes, naked and glistening with oil, entered the arena. Of all those who competed at the Games, these were the men who came the closest to the Greek ideal.[111] All-rounders, they had trained hard to achieve the height of physical perfection – a balanced strength in legs and arms and torso that would allow them to compete in such diverse activities

35. *Boxing, javelin, discus and running: four of the events of the pentathlon are watched over by a robed judge. Black-figure pottery, Athens, c.510–500 BC. Height 53.3 cm.*

as racing, jumping, throwing and close conflict.

As the young men, the flower of the Greek world, limbered up, the judges brought out the three official bronze discuses. These were stored for safe-keeping in the heart of the sanctuary, in the Treasury of the Sikyonians – a two-roomed building, itself lined in bronze, already over 200 years old, in which was also housed a golden-hilted sword said to have belonged to Pelops.[112]

The first of the athletes took his place within a strictly demarcated area, the *balbis,*

large enough for only one person to stand on, and then only with his the right leg. This forces the thrower to bend forward, putting no weight at all on his left leg; the left leg, then, must be straightened and brought forward at the same time as the right arm. The athlete holding the discus must turn his head to the right and bend over so far that he can look down at his side; he must throw the discus by pulling himself up and putting his whole right side into the throw.[113]

It was a standing throw, a swift unfurling of a supple body; a transfer of an athlete's weight designed to let the discus fly most swiftly. It seems that each man had three throws, one with each of the three discuses. One by one, the thin discs – each perhaps five pounds in weight, eight inches in diameter, and half an inch in thickness – spun through the air thudding dully on the dry parched soil. The furthest throw of all the three was marked with an identifying peg; then stewards ran forward to collect the discuses and carried them back (perhaps some 30 metres)[114] to the *balbis* where the next contestant waited. When all had thrown, to the full-throated cheers of the spectators from his city-state,

36. *Clutching dumbells in both hands and scrutinized by a judge, a long jumper swings back his arms to achieve momentum and a clean landing. Black-figure pottery, Athens, 540 BC. Height 42.2 cm.*

the winner was announced. One athlete had taken the crucial first step along the road to victory.

Next: the long jump. A landing-pit, the *skamma,* had already been prepared, more than sixteen metres in length; the sandy soil made soft with mattocks and raked smooth. Sixteen metres for one jump is impossible, and so it seems that the Olympic long jump was, in fact, a sequence of three jumps or more – three standing jumps, in which the landing was as crucial as the jump itself. If the athlete landed messily or fell, he was disqualified.[115]

To aid their jump, the athletes were equipped with weights, heavy dumbells, which they gripped, one in each hand. As he took

off, the jumper swung his arms in front of him with as much force as he could muster, the motion of the weights increasing his momentum. Then, as he came down, he swung his arms back rapidly again so that he might achieve the perfect balance and with it a clean landing.

For many spectators, the angle of whose view would be oblique, the difference in the distances involved would have been difficult to judge – only the reaction of the athletes to their jumps might have conveyed the outcome. It may have been partly for this reason, to add an extra dimension to the competition, that this was the only Olympic event to be accompanied by music. Tradition told of how the playing of the 'Pythian Melody for *Aulos*' – a reed instrument related to the *duduk* of Armenia or to the Western oboe –

had been 'introduced for the jump at the pentathlon, because the "Melody for *Aulos*" is sacred to Apollo, and Apollo won victories at Olympia.'[116]

Whatever the reason (and the Apollo explanation is patently not it), the musical accompaniment set the long jump curiously apart. Again, when all had jumped, the winner was announced. Now there was everything to play for – and the next two contests would be swiftly done. First: the javelin-throw. As with the discus, it seems that each contender could make three attempts, and it is again likely that, to ensure total fairness, official javelins were used. Each was roughly two metres long, fixed with a metal point, and with a throwing-loop, which the athlete attached onto the shaft just below the point of balance. The javelin-thrower slid his forefingers through the loop, the shaft resting lightly by his thumb, and at the moment of the throw, he used the tension of the loop to give the javelin extra impetus, sending it flying with a torsion which would carry it, its shaft rotating, straighter through the air. Again, after each set of three throws, the furthest was marked with a peg. Again, only one man could win.

By now, if an athlete had not come first at least one event, he had no hope of achieving the necessary goal of three wins. He had no choice but to retire, defeated, from the field. His fate and that of his fellow defeated athletes was, as the praise-singer Pindar imagined on a separate occasion, wretched:

> for them no joyous homecoming
> nor sweet laughter
>     to awaken joy

37. *A well-toned javelin thrower preens in a pose of relaxation. White-ground pottery, Athens, c.470 BC. Height 16 cm.*

38. *Grappling the torso, a wrestler tries to throw his resistant opponent. Black-figure pottery, Athens, c. 510–500 BC. Height 41.9 cm.*

> when they came home to their mothers
> no
> they slink along dark alleyways
>     avoiding their enemies
>     gnawed by failure.[117]

So now, as the tension mounted, the remaining athletes made their way to the far, eastern end of the stadium for the foot-race. Arriving at the starting line, they turned, and to the thunderous encouragement of every man there, crowded on the banks around them, took up their stance. For a moment, despite the noise and clamour, everything seemed frozen. Then the trumpet sounded, and the race began, and time rushed forward – muscles straining on their calves and thighs, their elbows bent, arms slicing, chests exploding with the surge of speed, eyes fixed firm on the finish, the athletes hurtled towards their goal. In a few short seconds it was done – the runners now bent double, gulping for their breath, sweat streaming down their faces and their bodies, but only one the victor.

If three men had taken part in the foot-race, perhaps only the first and second were allowed to go through to the last event of all: the crucial wrestling, 'the painful art'[118] as Homer had once called it. But about to be displayed was not the brute muscular force of the dedicated heavy wrestlers who would compete in two days' time (see p. 133f); rather these all-rounders, these pentathletes, were lighter, lither, faster on their feet. And yet the rules remained the same: to wrestle standing, upright, feet firmly on the ground; to grapple your opponent's torso; not to bite or gouge or punch, or twist their limbs to break them; trip them by all means, with leg or hand; or raise them from the ground and throw them down; but throw them anyway; for three clean throws ensured a victory.

The judges, trained in vigilance, aware of how much honour was at stake, each holding a long cane with which to strike an athlete (should he seem to break the rules), watched as the two men circled and then closed. Many of those watching would have remembered Homer's unrivalled description of the wrestling match, which was part of the funeral games of Patroclos:

> Great Ajax, son of Telamon, got to his feet, and up stood
> Odysseus, too, the crafty one, the guileful. The two men
> strode to the centre of the gathering and grasped one
> another with strong hands, tight like the tall rafters of a

building which a master craftsman has linked together to
protect him from the buffeting gale. Their backs creaked as
they strained with their strong hands and sweat dripped from
them as bruises purple with blood blossomed on chests and on
shoulders … Odysseus could not trip Ajax nor could Ajax
throw Odysseus, for Odysseus' strength held firm. When it
seemed the Greeks were growing restless, mighty Ajax son of
Telamon addressed Odysseus: 'God-born Odysseus, son of
Laertes, the guileful, either lift me up or I shall lift you; Zeus
will decide the outcome.' He lifted Odysseus up, but Odysseus
remembered his cunning. He kicked at Ajax where the knee-
back is hollow and loosened his limbs so he fell; and Odysseus
crashed on his chest and all the men watched him in wonder.
Then Odysseus too, the godlike, the suffering, tried to lift
Ajax. He raised him a little, but still could not lift him. His
knee gave way under him and so on the ground they fell hard
on each other and both men were stained with the dust …[119]

At last, exhausted, one of the two athletes fell for the third time.
The other stood, dazed, panting, sweating, but victorious, the
clamour of the crowds still echoing in his ears. For such an
athlete, nothing could come close to this: Olympic victory – at
home, the adulation of his city; throughout the Greek world,
praise, envy and undying fame.

   Clutching the victor's palm branch and borne aloft by his fellow
citizens, the winner was swept in triumph from the stadium,
while for his rival, defeated, shunned and scorned, there was
nothing left but broken pride. And so the crowds dispersed,
discussing the day's Games, back to their tents to change their
clothes and oil their hair in preparation for the sunset and the
rising of the full moon and for the solemn rites ahead.

CHAPTER 4

# HEROIC SACRIFICE; HEROIC CONTEST

## DAY 3 (FULL MOON)

Moonlight. Throughout the Altis and across the plain, shrines and statues, tents and trees and temples were bathed in a sharp-edged glow of silver-blue, while, all around, the silhouettes of mountains rose up black against the star-flecked sky. Already from the tents, sometimes in fluid groups of two or three, sometimes in tight-knit knots of chisel-faced and humourless young men, the entourages of the great and good of Greece, people were flocking to the Altis and the poplar-fringed enclosure, the Pelopion. For it was here that the first of this central day's two major ceremonies was soon to begin: the sacred rites in memory of Pelops.

With the full moon hanging high above them like a polished shield, they gathered at the entrance. This was on the western side of the enclosure, for, like all shrines dedicated to the dead, the way in to the Pelopion faced the setting sun. It was Heracles, they said, who first had venerated Pelops here, slaughtering a black ram at the sacred pit where he was buried; letting the blood pour deep into the earth, burning the ram's flesh on a sacred pyre so that the ghost of the dead hero might enjoy its scent.[120] For the Greeks, the boundary between the living and the dead was not impenetrable. Every year most cities held elaborate ceremonies to propitiate[121] the spirits of their ancestors, making ritual offerings to ghosts to turn aside their anger, knowing that the dead were jealous of the living and that, unless they were treated with respect, they could wreak unspeakable distress.

Something of the sense of awe surrounding such offerings is conveyed in Homer's *Odyssey*, when Odysseus himself describes the preparations he once made to commune with the dead. He found himself in a land of mist and cloud, a dark land of night, where the sun never shines:

> We reached the headland and beached the ship and unloaded the sheep and we walked by the waves of the Ocean till we came to the place we had heard of. There Perimedes and Eurylochos held down the sacrificial beasts while I drew my sharp sword from its place by my thigh and dug out a square pit, a cubit on each side, and poured in drink offerings to all of the dead: first was milk mixed with honey; then honey-sweet wine; and the third was pure water; and on top of it all I sprinkled white barley. Again and again I made vows to the strengthless heads of the dead that when I got home I would slaughter a sterile cow, the best in my herds, and pile high the pyre with my palace's riches. And I vowed to Teiresias for himself a fine ram, its fleece black, the best in my flocks. Now, when I had begged the tribes of the dead with my offerings and prayers, I brought forward the sheep and over the pit sliced their throats, and the black-clouding blood poured out from them, and the souls of the dead who had gone down to Hades collected before me ...[122]

It was a solemn moment, and for many, no doubt, one fraught with mystery and awe. The Olympic priests and officials took their positions by the sacrificial pit in the south-east of the

Pelopion. Beside them were the delegates and the ambassadors from all the panhellenic cities – representatives from every state in the Greek world – and thronged around them and outside the sacred compound, some watching from beyond the low stone wall, some lining the steps of the temples of Zeus and Hera, the thousands of others who had come to watch and wonder.

No full account survives of the specifics of the sacrifice, but much can be reconstructed. Libations[123] would be poured and prayers made, and as one of the priests forced the ram's head down towards the earth, so that its gaze might face the way its life-force was to travel, another brought the blade down heavy on its neck. Then, when the blood had coursed in sandy runnels and drained away into the dusty earth, the carcass was lifted up onto a pyre made solely from white poplar trees, and torches thrown upon it. Only the ram's neck would be eaten by a mortal man – a priest of Zeus known as the Woodsman, whose responsibility it was 'to provide timber for their sacrifices at a fixed price both to cities and to individuals'.[124] The rest of the meat was given to the ghost of Pelops, and the smoke from its burning, they believed, brought him sufficient joy that his anger or his jealousy, that they were still alive while he was not, might be averted.

Sixty years before (476 BC), the praise-singer Pindar had written of the sacrifice in a victory ode for Hieron, the tyrant of Syracuse, who had triumphed in the chariot race. Pelops, Pindar sang,

> is drenched in glorious offerings of blood
> by the crossing of the Alpheios at his tomb
> a place of pilgrimage by the altar
> where strangers throng past number.
> The fame of the Olympic Games, of Pelops' games,
> blazes over all the broad-backed earth.[125]

39. *Looking across the Pelopion today. The site of Pelops' altar, 'drenched in glorious blood offerings', was the scene of the first sacrifices of the Games' central day of the new moon.*

Perhaps he was echoing similar hymns sung by the gathered multitudes to propitiate the dead, as the fragrant smoke of sacrifice rose up, pale blue, into the moonlit sky. Of all the events which took place at Olympia, this was perhaps the most solemn – a moment of deep devotion; a descent to the threshold of the world of the dead. It made what was to follow all the more exuberant.

For this, too, was the evening when the first of the great victory banquets were held. These were hosted by private citizens, sometimes to mark their victory in the Games, and in 416 BC, it was to be an evening like no other. For this year, in a gesture unprecedented in all the history of the Olympic Games, one man

would undertake to provide food and drink and entertainment for every one of all the thousands who had come to celebrate the Festival. By now, there was no doubt of his identity: it was, of course, the winner of the chariot race the day before: Alcibiades.

Athenian drama deals in abstract absolutes. Of these perhaps the most well-known is *hubris*, the action or the state of mind which defines the moment when a tragic hero crosses the dividing line between what is acceptably within the bounds of human behaviour and what is not. Sometimes the word is translated as 'pride', but it means much more than that. It means a failure to recognize man's limitations. It means a blindness to accept what every sane person knows: that in all things is the potential for their opposite; that the dividing line between success and abject failure is thin as gossamer. There would be many who saw in this

lavish banquet on this sacred night of the full moon the moment, not only of Alcibiades' *hubris* but of the *hubris* of his city, Athens. As ever, Alcibiades did it in style.

It was an act of personal and political propaganda on a colossal scale. Again, it involved those richest of the eastern islands, Chios and Lesbos, for (as well as providing fodder for his horses) the citizens of Chios had contributed vast flocks of sheep and herds of cattle to be sacrificed and then eaten at Alcibiades' banquet, while the islanders of Lesbos 'sent wine and other supplies for all the lavish entertainments which he hosted'.[126] But it was not only foreign city-states which contributed to the event. For the feast was distributed and consumed from plates and vessels of pure gold and silver, 'borrowed' from the vaults of the state treasuries of Athens.[127] It was a naked statement of pure power – the power of Athens, but more obviously the power of Alcibiades himself.

It must have provoked some quite extraordinary reactions, not only among Athens' rivals but among her allies and her citizens themselves. We do not know who else from Athens attended these Olympic Games of 416 BC, but it is highly likely that (in either an official or a personal capacity) many of her leading generals and politicians were there. They possibly included men like Nikias, the elder statesman, who had negotiated peace with Sparta five years earlier, only to have the treaty seriously jeopardized by Alcibiades' underhand treatment of some Spartan diplomats. Recently Nikias had been forced to enter into a political pact with Alcibiades, but he still mistrusted him.[128] Perhaps, too, Andocides was there, a demagogue who hated Alcibiades and would later bring him down (see p. 189).[129] Perhaps the majority of the elite of Athens were

(see p. 189)

40. *Reclining on a couch, a banqueter raises his wine cup in his right hand. Red-figure pottery, Athens, 490–480 BC. Height 9 cm.*

most like those, who, Plutarch later claimed, 'did not appear to be
his enemies, but really hated him no less than those who openly
declared it.'[130] Such was the strength of feeling Alcibiades aroused.

Among those from other cities, opinion was equally divided.
Clearly there were some, like the aristocrats from Chios and
Lesbos, who believed that, by allying themselves to Alcibiades,
they were likely to further their own causes, both political and
economic. Others, like the delegation from Segesta in the east of
Sicily, hoped that he would help provide military aid. For, at some
time during the Olympic Festival, there may have been meetings,
conducted in the utmost secrecy, in which the Segestans had
discussed with Alcibiades the possibility of Athens sending a
military task force to Sicily, ostensibly at least to help them in a
war against their neighbouring state, Selinus. They may have
pointed out that, with a toehold on the island, it would then be

41. *The marriage of Peleus and Thetis: Strife's lack of an invitation to their (mythical) banquet
gave rise to the Trojan War. Black-figure pottery, Athens, c. 580–570 BC. Height 71 cm.*

possible for Athens to turn her attention to the conquest of that richest of all western cities, Syracuse, and once they'd conquered Syracuse, the wealth and harvest of all Sicily would be in Athens' (or perhaps in Alcibiades' own) hands ...

And then there were Athens' avowed enemies: Thebes and Corinth, Megara and Sparta. How they reacted to this act of showmanship from Alcibiades can only be imagined. Divisive as always, with this banquet a paean[131] to his own ego, Alcibiades had smashed the thin Olympic veneer of panhellenic unity and, like the goddess Strife who brought the golden apple to the wedding feast of Peleus and Thetis and so provoked the Trojan War,[132] he had introduced dissension where none should have been.

With daylight, though, the balance was restored. For now the uneasy night was over, and with it the banquets and the rituals to the dead. The sun had risen, its radiance outshining even the full moon. On this central morning of the Festival, it was time to honour the greatest god of all, Olympian Zeus. For much, if not all of the Games' history, this arrangement of liturgy and worship contained the key to the inner meaning of the Festival: rites to a dead hero done in darkness, followed by an extravagance of sacrifice to the supreme sky god performed in the bright light of day, the two united by the luminescence of the full August moon. It was a pattern followed elsewhere too – at Eleusis, for example, where rituals enacting the great mysteries of death and rebirth culminated in an ecstatic celebration of life.

With dawn, the priests and delegates, the athletes and spectators gathered – perhaps before the Prytaneum (see p. 129f) in the north-east quadrant of the Altis. Not only was this the administrative centre for the sanctuary, it was here that the sacred flame was kept alive on the altar of Hestia (see p. 131); and from this flame every fire which burned on every altar in the Altis was lit.[133] It was a solemn ceremony, accompanied by the pouring of libations and the singing of ancient hymns, whose words the traveller Pausanias had heard, though he would not reveal them.[134] Today was no exception, so, with the lighting ceremony done and with torches blazing, ready to ignite the great inferno on the altar, all was ready for the short procession which would skirt the low walls of the Pelopion until it came to the tall ash mound at the very heart of the sanctuary of Olympia. At the head of the procession were the dignitaries from Elis, for this event was their domain, and, close behind, the sacrificial victims: a hundred oxen, chosen for their strength and their perfection, their coats gleaming, their horns glinting in the morning sun. Great care was taken to ensure that the animals were perfect and unblemished and that they seemed to go willingly to slaughter. Accompanied, no doubt, by musicians, the procession set off, the richest men among them proudly dressed in sumptuous robes and garlanded with flowers.

Their destination was the great altar of Zeus, the most sacred place in all the sanctuary. Here, a low rectangular base, raised from the earth by a shallow flight of steps, was topped by a mound of white compacted ash. By Pausanias' day (second century AD), the mound was seven metres high, with steps cut into it for access to the highest point. In 416 BC it must have been considerably lower – for what made the mound extraordinary was that every year, albeit imperceptibly, it grew. For it was continually added to, constructed as it was from the burnt ashes of the bones of oxen offered up in sacrifice to Zeus. Pausanias explains: 'Each year the prophets, keeping strictly to the nineteenth day of the Month of the Deer,[135] carry ash from the Prytaneum, and mixing it with water, paste it onto the altar.'[136]

Now, when they reached the altar, the attendants led the oxen up the low ramp to the 'outer circle'.[137] Here, as the congregation looked on from below, barley was scattered over the oxen's heads and water trickled onto their foreheads – a sacramental act of preparation. Then, when all was ready, the priests brought out the sharpened sacrificial knives, and with one deft movement raised each ox's head, so that its eyes looked high towards the heavens, and as he did so sliced the creature's throat. A hundred slashes of a hundred knives, and one by one a hundred oxen collapsed onto their knees in the last throes of death.

Swiftly the priests butchered the still steaming carcasses. The rest of the meat they heaped on platters to be taken back to the Prytaneum, but the legs they carried reverentially up the ash-cut steps to where a pyre had been erected at the altar's top. Again, only white poplar branches could be used to feed the sacred fire, and when all the legs of all the oxen had been placed carefully in position, the torch-bearer climbed up to the high platform and set light to the pyre. As the dry wood caught, the flames leapt up and the poplar smoke mingled with the smoke from the sputtering and crackling meat and fat and bones, in an aroma to delight Olympian Zeus.

There were two miraculous phenomena associated with this altar, both of which demonstrated just how dear it was to Zeus. The first was that kites and other birds of prey never tried to snatch the sacrificial meat away from it – something which, had it happened, would have been considered to be extremely ill-omened.[138] The second was that both the area round the altar and, indeed, the entire Altis itself was oddly free of flies. Flies, of course, were constantly attracted to places of animal slaughter, and could be a nuisance.

According to legend, however, when Heracles was sacrificing at Olympia he was plagued by clouds of flies. So either because the idea came to him himself or because someone suggested it, he sacrificed to Zeus Who Banishes Flies (Zeus Apomuios), and so the flies were banished to the other side of the Alpheios. They say that, following his example, the

men of Elis sacrifice to Zeus Who Banishes Flies in order to drive flies away from Olympia. [139]

With its prayers and hymns and incense, the great hecatomb[140] to Zeus was, for the briefest moment, an affirmation of unity among Greek-speaking states – an acknowledgement of a common heritage and shared beliefs. It was one of the few times when men from every city-state from the entire Greek world could stand truly shoulder to shoulder in a communion of purpose, as they acknowledged the supremacy of the greatest god whose worship they all shared, Olympian Zeus.

The ceremony over, it was time for each of the delegations from the city-states to make their own sacrifices on their own behalf. Some were perhaps conducted at the great altar itself, others at the many lesser altars to Zeus which were scattered throughout the Altis. It was for these sacrifices that the Woodman had cut, dried, stored and sold the stocks of white poplar,[141] a delicate exercise no doubt not only in logistics but in diplomacy. For a few hours, then, the sanctuary resounded to the clomp of oxen's hooves as they were led to sacrifice; to the shrill bray of the *aulos* and the singing of the hymns, as smoke and incense rose up high into the warm August air. And with them rose the prayers of men.

42. *A bull is led to sacrifice, a scene repeated hundreds of times on the morning of the central day of the Olympic Festival. Plaster cast of south metopé from the Parthenon, Athens.*

By midday all was over. The delegates and the spectators had returned to their tents to change out of their ceremonial robes and the meat from the oxen was being prepared for the coming feast. But before any banqueting took place, there were races to be run, and among them the most important and most ancient of all of the events held at Olympia: the running of the stade (a distance of approximately 200 metres).

Legend told that, when the Olympic Festival was first inaugurated in 776 BC, the stade race was the only athletic event in which competitors took part. Whether this is historically true or not, when it is unpacked, the legend reveals several important details: that the first festivals were considered to be predominately religious events, in which, in terms of time at least, the sporting element formed but a small part;[142] and that in the beginning it was a relatively local event. Indeed, it was not until well over a century and a half later, in the early sixth century BC, that Olympia began to attract participants from the rest of the Greek world and so could consider itself to be truly panhellenic.[143]

The other important detail which the legend gives us is the name of the winner of the first race: Koroibos, who came (appropriately enough) from nearby Elis. Such was the importance placed on it, that the names of every winner in every stade race of every Olympic Games from then on were recorded and disseminated. Indeed, thanks to Eusebius (c. AD 260–340), the bishop of Caesarea,[144] we still have a complete list of victors in the stade race, which stretches over a thousand years from 776 BC to AD 254. That we still have this information is thanks, in part, to a flamboyant character who was in all probability present at our Games of 416 BC, a local man from Elis, the self-styled genius and polymath, the sophist Hippias.

Much of what we know about Hippias comes from hostile sources, chief among which are the two dialogues which bear his name, purportedly by Plato. In these we hear of his towering intellectual vanity, which not only led him to believe that he was capable of discoursing with equal authority on any topic from politics to poetry or from art to rhetoric, but which (usefully for him) enabled him to persuade others to part with large sums of money for the privilege of being taught by him. Naturally, one of the most profitable forums for someone like Hippias – a place where he could most readily demonstrate his abilities to the largest possible audience, while at the same time attracting more potential students – was the Olympic Games, where we hear of him 'delighting Greece with his carefully-wrought speeches'.[145] Here, his appearance was flamboyant. Addressing him in one of Plato's dialogues, Socrates (who, shunning travel, probably never attended the Olympic Festival) exclaims:

> You claimed once, when you went to Olympia, that you had yourself made everything that you were wearing. I begin, as you did, with your ring – you were expert in engraving rings; another ring, your seal-ring, was your work, too; and your scraper, and an oil-flask. Then you spoke of how you had made your sandals and woven your robe and tunic. Then – and this was what everyone thought most remarkable, the ultimate proof of your wisdom – you told everyone how the sash on your tunic was identical to the most expensive of all sashes worn by Persians, and that you had made it yourself! As if that was not enough, you had brought along your

43. **Overleaf:** *Raising its head so that it gazes towards the sky, winged Victory herself prepares to sacrifice an ox. Terracotta, Italy, c. 50 BC–AD 50. Height 25.4 cm.*

44. *Today nothing remains of the great ashen altar of Zeus, but it was close to the Temple of Zeus, seen here among the trees.*

poetry, epics and tragedies, and dithyrambs, not to mention prose writings on a multitude of topics. You were pre-eminent, you said, in all these arts, as well as in rhythm and harmony and …[146]

The list goes on. But what Plato fails to recount is the fact that it was Hippias who devised a universal method of chronology. Before Hippias, each city had used its own way of identifying any given year, usually from the name of its chief magistrate. This was all well and good (if a little clumsy) if all one wanted to do was recall local history. But for someone trying to compile a wider

chronicle, it could lead to all sorts of confusion. Hippias' answer was to introduce a system of dating, which became accepted throughout the Greek-speaking world, based on Olympiads. Thus 776 BC became 'the year of the first Olympiad, at which Koroibos of Elis won the stade'; 772 BC 'the year of the second Olympiad at which Antimakhos of Elis won the stade' and so on. The intervening years were then numbered accordingly, with 775 BC, being known as the second year of the first Olympiad.

This new system of chronology, of course, had another significant effect. It gave even more prominence than before to the winner of that oldest race of all, the stade. For, after Hippias, the athlete who first crossed the line would always be remembered whenever anyone anywhere wrote or spoke of the history of his times. It was as close to immortality as he might hope to come.

But first came the *dolikhos*. Introduced in 720 BC, this was a trial not so much of speed but of endurance. At just over four and a half kilometres[147] it was the longest of all Olympic races, requiring the athletes to cover 24 lengths of the stadium. With their slender legs and muscular necks and shoulders,[148] for most of the race the *dolikhos* runners kept themselves in check, pounding the course rhythmically, arms bent, fists clenched, keeping bunched up close together. Only in the final strait would they begin to sprint, lengthening their stride, pummelling their arms, throwing back their heads as, in a final spurt of pure adrenalin, they coursed the last few metres to the winning line.

It was a feat of stamina, yet there were some *dolikhos* winners who, even after the race was run, still possessed remarkable reserves of energy. We hear of two men who, elated at their win, resolved to bear the news of victory back to their home cities before sunset the next day. So, in 328 BC, Ageus ran 60 miles across the mountains of Arcadia to tell his fellow citizens in Argos of his success, while later Drymos ran 80 miles to Epidaurus to be the first to report his victory to the townsfolk there. An inscription, which records his feat, survives.[149]

But now, even as the winner of the *dolikhos* was being hailed, and as the ribbon of his victory was being tied around his head, far over at the eastern side of the vast stadium, the sprinters were already limbering up. In the first century AD, the Roman poet Statius described such a scene. Before the race, he writes (in typically purple verse), the runners

> practise their speed and hone their paces, and by many skills
> and feigned elation awake their torpid limbs; now they kneel
> knees-bent, now loudly strike their well-oiled chests, now
> exercise their fiery feet in short sprints and in sudden stops.[150]

Now it was only those who had survived the heats who could take their position at the starting line.[151] With the embanked slopes of the stadium packed tight on either side with partisan spectators, their anticipation stretched to breaking point, each runner stood there, naked and impatient, ready for the off, but each wary of making a false start. For each man knew the penalty

45. Dolikhos *runners settle into a steady stride for their race of just over four and a half kilometres. Black-figure pottery, Athens, 333–332* BC. *Height 67.3 cm.*

46. *'Breath on the back of the head': Two sprinters race for the finishing line. Black-figure pottery, Athens, c. 510–500 BC. Height 53.3 cm.*

if he did: a whipping with long canes by the enforcers of the rules, the *Alytes*.[152] That and disqualification. There could be no ending more humiliating for the athlete.

So, tense and ready, one foot forward, toes taut, back foot pressing hard on the hard ground, and all the time the feeling of the warm earth rising up beneath them; chest forward, chin up, elbows bent, hands flat and fingers flexing, the runners waited in the August sun and listened for the trumpet.

And then it came. The race was on. Like a volley of arrows the runners shot from the starting line – so Statius describes the scene,[153] and grasping for another simile he adds they ran: 'like stags, which hear or think they hear a lion roar, hungry, far away, and panic drives them on in blind and terrifying flight.' Close to each other, not a hair's breadth separating them.

Those watching might have thought of the great scene in Homer's *Iliad*, when the heroes ran in honour of the dead Patroclos. Ajax was ahead

> but godlike Odysseus pressed close on him, as close as to a
> woman's breast the shuttle, when in her expert hands she
> draws the thread and stretches it out and along the warp.
> Close to her breast she holds it. And just as close Odysseus
> ran – but at his back, and his feet were pounding Ajax's
> tracks before the dust settled. Godlike Odysseus was
> breathing down his rival's neck, as he kept up his swift pace,
> and all the Greeks were cheering as he strove for victory,
> roaring their support as he kept running.[154]

For the shortest of times, the outcome hung poised in the balance. Then the final spurt of speed. A blur of legs and feet, and one man crossed the line ahead of all the others. The *Hellanodikai* whose task it was to stand there by the finish had all seen him win. The judgement was secure. His victory was proclaimed, the ribbon tied around his head in triumph, the palm branch pressed into his hand; his fellow citizens all hoarse now in their frenzy as they shouted their support, for no one was in any doubt that he had won: Exainetus of Acragas.[155] His was the name which would forever be associated in their minds and in the minds of all the

Greeks with this, the 91st Olympiad.

Not only with the 91st Olympiad. Four years later (412 BC), when he returned, Exainetus once more ran home to victory in the stade race. This time, the citizens of Acragas were doubly overjoyed. They heroized Exainetus. When his ship docked at the harbour back in Sicily he was met by cheering crowds.

> He was escorted into the city in a chariot — three hundred other chariots, each drawn by two white horses, went with him in procession, and all the chariots belonged to citizens of Acragas.[156]

It was a city known for luxury. Its vine-yards and its olive groves, its temples and its fish-ponds – all were famous. Its people wore the finest and most delicate of robes, with golden ornaments and perfumed hair. And though it remained untouched and neutral in the war which Athens waged in Sicily, in 406 BC a Carthaginian army came and sacked it. Perhaps Exainetus fell fighting for his city. We do not know. By then he had passed out of history.

47. *A triumph of experience over youth: two bearded runners outstrip their younger beardless rivals. Black-figure pottery, Athens, 510–500 BC. Height 53 cm.*

On that August day of 416 BC there was still one more race to run: the diaulos – the double stade – in which the athletes started at the western limit of the track, their backs towards the temple and the great altar of Zeus. If it was in part eclipsed by the prestige of the stade race, it was not the less exciting. The runners sprinted hard down to the eastern end, then, when their feet touched the stone marker, sunk deep into the dusty earth, they turned and raced the final length back to the finish. The turn was all important. If the athlete slipped and fell, then all was lost. If he appeared to interfere with one of his adversaries, he could be disciplined and then, again, all would be lost. A clean turn was the key, that and no loss of speed. And then the lightning dash towards the dipping sun, the temples silhouetted dark against the sky; the runners' shadows lengthened on the churned-up track behind them, their faces gold in the late summer light.

So, with the last race run and the last victor's name proclaimed, the last event of this, the central day was over and the crowds dispersed – some, like the citizens of Acragas, elated at their fellow townsman's win, others feeling possibly detached or even perhaps angry that the runner on whom all their hopes had been so firmly pinned had failed them. Yet all were united in one thought: of the ritual meal to come. For, while the races were being run and the spectators had been cheering on their champions, back in the tents and in the Prytaneum the carcasses of oxen and the other sacrificial beasts were being butchered and the tender meat prepared, and, as the sun sank ever lower in the west, the fragrant scent of cooking drifted tantalizingly across the plain.

CHAPTER 5

# BLOOD ON THE SAND

## DAY 4 (FULL MOON PLUS ONE)

Official banquets can be tedious events. Their main purpose is often nothing more than to allow the hosts an opportunity to feel important. Often enough, this means requiring guests to dress up in unusually formal clothing, to sit where they are told to sit, to make small talk with those they would rather not speak to at all, and to listen to interminable self-congratulatory speeches. There is no reason to suppose that the official banquet, held this evening in the Prytaneum at Olympia and hosted by those members of the Elean establishment who had been responsible for organizing this year's games, was any different.

Only the elite would be invited to attend. For the rest, the rich and powerful could console themselves by staging their own state banquets, each with its own etiquette and hierarchy; each allowing the hosts to display their largesse to members of their own community (and thus to help them win political support). For one city, this year's banquet involved an unwelcome irritation. The day before, Alcibiades had appropriated Athens' official gold and silver plate from which to serve the largesse of his own feast. Now many people, seeing it reused at the Athenian state dinner quite naturally assumed that, as they had seen it first being used by Alcibiades, it must belong to him, and he must have loaned it for the day to Athens. It was the sort of situation which

Alcibiades, reclining in the Prytaneum, must have relished.

All the banquets – the one hosted by the Elean authorities and all the state banquets being enjoyed across the plain – were the convenient by-product of the morning's sacrifices, for, as befitted so practical a people as the Greeks, religious ritual managed to combine the making of a pious offering to gods with the enjoyment of more earthly pleasures. Conveniently, they consecrated that part of the animal which was inedible, while they themselves feasted on the rest. The myths, which had sprung up in explanation of this expedient phenomenon, tell us much about mankind's perceived relationship with the gods – and in particular with the great god Zeus himself. The early poet Hesiod tells the myth of how one of the first of the new race of mortals, Prometheus, succeeded in tricking the gods:

> There was a judgement once at Mekone between gods and
> mortal men when, with a leaping heart Prometheus
> apportioned a great ox and sought to deceive the mind of
> Zeus. Before the others he laid out the meat, the fat and
> marbled offal and the hid them in the belly of the ox.But
> before Zeus he laid the white ox bones, arranged with skill
> and hidden in rich shining folds of fat … Prometheus of the
> crooked mind smiled soft and said: 'Zeus, you most glorious
> and greatest of the gods who live for ever, take one of these,
> whichever one the spirit in your breast delights in.' He said
> this to deceive, but Zeus who understands immortal plans
> was not deceived. He understood the ruse, and in his heart
> devised cruel punishments for mortal men in days to come.
> In both his hands he took the portion wrapped in the
> white fat but his mind was angered and in his heart he
> raged to see the white bones of the ox, Prometheus' trick.

And from that day, upon the earth the tribes of men burn
white bones on their smoking altars.[157]

Hesiod cannot quite manage to imagine that the omniscient
Zeus could really have been tricked in such a way, and yet he still
must make Zeus choose the lesser portion. But of even greater
interest is the relationship between the strongest of the gods and
man. Prometheus shows no subservience. Rather he uses his wits
and cunning to get the better of a powerful being who, at this
moment, is his adversary. This episode describes nothing less than
a contest in which, as always, the winner takes everything. Its
spirit is the same as that of the Olympic Games. No matter who
or what it is, with whom one is competing, one should at all times
aim to win. If the odds are stacked against you, it makes winning
all the sweeter. This was the philosophy, too, by which the
political leaders played, those men who, dressed now in the
richest and most dazzling of clothes, their heads garlanded with
flowers perhaps grown specially for this occasion, made their way
through the moonlit Altis to the Prytaneum.

Sadly and frustratingly, very little survives of the Prytaneum as
it was in the late fifth century BC. Later Roman rebuilds and
subsequent destruction saw to that. What we do know, though,
suggests a fine imposing structure, thirty-three metres square,
with a colonnaded portico, cool and elegant, running round the
outside, while within was an open cloistered courtyard. At the
heart of the complex was a room, seven metres square, which
contained the inner sanctuary and the altar of Hestia, with its
ever-burning flame, from which the torches for the sacrificial
fires had, only that morning, been lit (see p. 111). In another part
of the building, perhaps in the capacious northern colonnade,
were the official reception rooms, in which the Olympic banquet

would take place. These, too, would have been decked in style, with carved and precious couches, costly furnishings and garlands strung between the pillars, all dancing in the flickering torchlight. There would undoubtedly have been musicians, female *aulos*-players perhaps,[158] and singers and performers on the lyre.[159] Such are the details we can sketch from references to other banquets in contemporary literature or from scenes shown in vase-paintings. Perhaps we can take heart from the realization that, for most of those attending the Olympic Festival, all they could do was similarly speculate about what happened at this banquet. To them, like us, the doors were closed and, like us, they would have to wait until the morning before they could rejoin the official schedule.

If being excluded from the banquet might breed frustration, then the contests which now lay ahead were the perfect forum in which that frustration might be channelled. For this, already the last day of the Festival on which games would be held, was the day of the most violent contact sports in the Greek world: the wrestling and boxing and, arguably the most brutal of them all, the pankration (see p. 150f.); and to round off not this day alone

48. *Accompanied by a performer on the double aulos, and with a ladle-bearing slave on hand, ivy-wreathed banqueters indulge their appetites. Red-figure pottery, Athens, 490–480* BC. *Diameter 31.9 cm.*

but the entire Olympic Games, a martial race by athletes in armour.

The spectators had, of course, already seen two bouts of wrestling: one in the pentathlon two days earlier, the other in the boys' events on the first day. But in both these cases the contestants' strength was not quite fully developed: the boys had not yet reached maturity, whereas the pentathletes were all-rounders – men who could run and jump and throw the discus or the javelin as well as they could wrestle.[160] Today, however, the crowds would see the specialists – some of the strongest men alive. And all of them meant business. Around many of them legends soon sprang up, but still the greatest reputation clung to Milo (see p. 65). He, it was said, had been so strong that he had carried his own victory statue single-handed into the Altis; 'could stand on an oiled discus and laugh as people hurled themselves against him and tried to push him off'; and regularly gave demonstrations of his strength in which 'he kept his right elbow by his side and held out his forearm straight to the front with the hand turned thumb uppermost and fingers flat; yet no one could shift his little finger'.[161] When men like this came into the

wrestling ground (see p. 101), their opponents surely shuddered.

It was in 708 BC that wrestling had been introduced into the Games, and in the intervening centuries the rules had not changed. We have already seen them observed in the pentathlon (see p. 101). Naked, oiled and doused in sand, they stood, the sixteen or so contestants who would grapple with each other in the morning sun to see which one of them would win the olive wreath.[162] The first hurdle to be passed was the drawing of the

49. *A forest of columns marks out the large inner courtyard of the third-century BC palaistra, where athletes trained in boxing, wrestling and the pankration.*

lots to find who, in the first round, would fight whom. It was not unknown for a contender to withdraw when he discovered who he would be up against. In such a case, his adversary automatically went through to the next round.[163] Indeed, one of the stories told of Milo was that he had once intimidated all the other wrestlers so much that no one was prepared to enter into combat with him, so he had won without even having to fight.[164]

There are no tales of Milo having to resort to underhand techniques, but others did. Earlier in the century,[165] Leontiskos,

50. 'Grasp his head in your right arm!' A powerful wrestler fights by the rules. Bronze. Roman, first century BC to first century AD. Height 12.7 cm.

the so-called Bone-Cracker from the Sicilian town of Messene had exploited a loophole in the rules and perfected a devastating technique, bending back his opponents' fingers until the pain was such that they conceded defeat.

One by one, on the raked earth east of the two temples and the great ash altar, where crowds cheered or sighed or winced to see the pain etched in faces so determined not to lose, the wrestlers fell, until at last there were only two. Like great bulls they would circle one another, looking for some weakness; seeking to intimidate; trying to trip the other before crashing heavily upon him; striving always to be the last man standing. As in the previous bouts, it was the best of five falls. If your adversary fell three times, you then won.

A fragment of a training manual found in Egypt gives a flavour of the types of moves the wrestlers employed:

> Stand beside him. Grasp his head in your right arm.
> At him! Go behind him. Take him from below. Power
> through. At him! Duck beneath his right arm. Grasp that arm
> and hook your left leg over his thigh. Throw him across your
> left leg. At him! Spin round. Grab both his legs. At him!
> Right foot forward. Throw your arms around his torso.
> Power forward. Bend him back. Face forward and push back
> against him ...[166]

Who the champion in 416 BC was, we do not know. His name is unrecorded. But of a winner, 28 years earlier, we do hear, and his story introduces us to some of the strange tales that would surround these strong men of the Games. In 444 BC, when Taurosthenes (whose name, or nickname, means 'Bull-Strength') won the wrestling match, an apparition of the athlete appeared

51. *Blood streaming from his nose, a boxer battles on. Black-figure pottery, Athens, c.550–540 BC. Height 21.6 cm.*

that very day to his fellow citizens in Aegina to tell them he had won.[167] (The Roman author, Aelian, has an equally intriguing if more rational version of how this victory was reported. According to him,[168] Taurosthenes sent back the news by homing pigeon. A purple cloth tied to its leg told of his win.)

Of all the contact sports this day, the wrestling was the least bloody, but with only three more contests of the 91st Olympics remaining, things would become distinctly more violent. For now, as the August sun was climbing to its highest point and its heat to its most merciless, the time had come for boxing. Only the most wealthy families could afford the fees that the top trainers might command, so here in the boxing contest, on the tamped sand of Olympia, the naked power of bodily strength met the more subtle power of money. The stakes could not be higher. The glory for the winner was incalculable.

There were no rounds, no formal chances to recover or draw breath; no end was possible until one of the boxers had subdued the other. Almost any blow was sanctioned: hooks and cuts and punches, chops with the side of the hand, thrusts with the open palm. Even when a man was on the floor, until he had conceded defeat or the judges intervened to stop the fight, he was fair game. As the spectators, eager for blood, were kept back by the officials so that enough space might be made, the boxers and the purple-robed referees entered the *ad hoc* arena.

What did they look like, these ancient boxers? In his book *On Gymnastics,* written in the second century AD, the Athenian Philostratus tells us that they

> should have a long hand, strong forearms and powerful
> upper arms, broad shoulders and a long neck. Thick wrists
> strike stronger blows, but thinner ones are flexible and strike
> more readily. He should have solid hips for support – the
> momentum of his striking out will cause him to lose balance
> if his torso is not anchored on firm hips. I regard fat calves as
> worthless in every sport … A boxer's form is better for
> attack if his thighs do not come together. The best boxer has
> a small belly, for he is nimble and has good breath control.
> On the other hand, a big belly gives some advantage to the
> boxer, as it gets in the way of the opponent who is aiming
> for the face.[169]

How seriously we are meant to take this last remark is anybody's guess. The image of a portly boxer certainly would seem to fly in the face of what we read elsewhere. More recognizable is this description by Theocritus of the mythical boxer Amycus:

> A giant of a man was sitting in the sun, a terrifying sight.
> His ears were crushed from boxing; his massive chest and
> broad back bulged with muscles; his flesh was like iron; his
> body like a mighty statue hammered out of metal; on his
> upper arms his muscles swelled beneath the shoulders, like
> mighty rocks scraped and polished by a winter torrent in full
> rushing spate.[170]

Theocritus' account of Amycus' encounter with the Spartan
Polydeuces is no doubt based on his own observations of real-life
boxing contests. The description is not for the faint-hearted:

> In the midst of the gathering the two men met, and both
> breathed out murder. Each circled the other as each strove
> to see which man could get the blinding sun behind him.
> Skilfully, Polydeuces ducked past the huge man and the sun
> struck Amycus full in his face. In fury, Amycus closed in on
> him, aiming a blow but Polydeuces sidestepped and struck
> him full square on the chin. More furious than ever, the
> other flailed out ...

> Light on his feet, Polydeuces hit out at him, now with this
> fist now with the other, stopping Amycus dead in his tracks
> in spite of his stature.

> The towering man swayed on his feet now, drunk with the
> punches, and spitting dark blood. And all the spectators were
> cheering. They could see the deep cuts round his mouth and
> his jaws, how his eyes too were narrowing, how his face

swelled with bruises. Polydeuces kept on confusing him, feinting and lunging from every direction.

When he knew that his rival was utterly helpless he landed a blow where the nose meets the eyebrows, and exposed all the bone of his forehead. Amycus crashed back in the leaves on the earth ... Blood was belching from his gaping temple. Polydeuces smashed his opponent's mouth; teeth rattled loose; again and again he landed his punches, each one more heavy; he pummelled the face so the cheeks caved in.

52. *Two powerfully built boxers contend for the prize of a palm branch, held by the goddess Athene, their judge. Black-figure pottery, Athens, c. 336 BC. Height 83.8 cm.*

Then at last, dazed, Amycus, slumped on the ground, raised his hand in surrender. He was very near death.[170]

At the Olympics of 416 BC, the fight was not meant to result in death. The boxers were all too aware that, if they killed their opponent, the chances were that they themselves would be disqualified – and the prize awarded to the dead man. This is not to say that death never occurred. Some years later, an infamous (and hotly debated) contest at the Nemean Games[171] dragged on so long that the two fighters, Kreugas of Epidamnus (modern Durrës in Albania) and Damoxenos of Syracuse, were told by the judges to decide the match by landing alternate undefended blows upon each other, a common way of bringing a long fight to its conclusion.

Kreugas aimed his punch at Damoxenos' head. Damoxenos then ordered Kreugas to lift up his arm; when Kreugas did this, Damoxenos slammed his hand with his fingers held straight out right under

53. *A pankratist raises his finger to concede defeat (too late?) as his opponent prepares to land a deadly blow. Black-figure pottery, Athens, 515–500 BC. Height 44.5 cm.*

Kreugas' ribs. With the sharpness of his fingernails and the force of his blow, he drove his hand deep into Kreugas' guts. He grabbed the bowels and tore them out and Kreugas died where he fell.[172]

Inevitably death had occurred at Olympia, too. In one Games, Diognetus of Crete, was not only disqualified but attacked by the crowd, because the challenger he had killed shared the name of their patron hero: Heracles.[173] In another, at the 74th Olympiad of 484 BC, Kleomedes, a boxer from the Aegean island of Astypalaia, killed his opponent and, when the judges disqualified him, he went mad. What happened next was chilling and its eventual outcome, to the modern mind at least, bizarre. Kleomedes sailed back to his beautiful island home where

he attacked a school where there were about sixty boys: he tore down the pillar that held up the roof, and the roof collapsed on top of them. The citizens pelted him with rocks but he took refuge in the sanctuary of Athene. He climbed inside a chest which was inside the shrine, and closed the lid. The people of Astypalaia struggled in vain to open it; at last they smashed the wood in, but they found no trace of Kleomedes either alive or dead. So they sent to Delphi to ask what had happened to him, and, according to them, the priestess gave them this oracle: Astypalaian Kleomedes is the last hero. Worship him. He is no longer mortal.[174]

To us, the idea of worshipping someone who has been responsible for a school massacre is repugnant. To the Greeks, however, to be mad was to be touched by the gods. Indeed, incidents of madness run like a pulsing vein through many stories of Olympic boxers –

54. *A reminder of the primitive: a warrior takes leave of his beloved before going out to fight a hero (see p. 148). Red-figure pottery, Campania, c.470–424 BC. Height 30.5 cm.*

men like Timanthes from Kleonai, a town not far from Nemea. Having retired from boxing, he nonetheless kept fit by bending 'an enormous bow each day. For a time he was away from home and gave up exercising with the bow; when he came home and found himself incapable of bending the bow, he kindled a great fire and threw himself onto it alive.'[175] In doing so he was

dramatically re-enacting the death of the great Olympic hero, the archer Heracles, who, cursed and in torment, had died in the flames of his self-made pyre.

It was perhaps inevitable that such huge personalities should attract to themselves a folklore all of their own. The strangest and the one which more than any makes the flesh crawl is the story of Euthymus. Purporting to have happened a generation before our Games, it is worth recounting in full, as it takes us into a mindset far removed from our own and reminds us, if we need reminding, how very different from us the ancient Greeks were. It was in 476 BC, at the 76th Olympics, that Euthymus won the boxing. He came from Lokris, a city in southern Italy. In a seemingly innocent sentence, Pausanias tells us: 'When Euthymus went back to Italy, he fought the Hero.' But when he explains who (or what) the 'Hero' was, an explanation which takes us back into the world of legend, the story takes a sinister twist:

They say that, while wandering after the fall of Troy, Odysseus was carried by storms to various cities in Italy and Sicily; one of these, to which he came with his was Temesa. Here, a member of his crew got drunk and raped a virgin girl. The people of Temesa stoned him to death for his crime. As for Odysseus, he was unmoved by man's death and sailed away. But the daemonic spirit of the man they had stoned to death kept on killing the Temesans, attacking old

55. *Holding a palm branch in his right hand and an olive wreath in his left, a judge watches a contest's dying moments. Black-figure pottery, Athens, 332–331 BC. Height 77 cm.*

and young alike. In time, they wanted to abandon Temesa and leave Italy for good, but the Delphic priestess would not let them go; instead, she ordered them to propitiate the Hero, by constructing a sacred enclosure, building a temple, and offering him each year the most beautiful virgin in Temesa to be his wife. They did as the god had commanded them, and the daemonic spirit ceased to trouble them.

So far, so mythological; now, however, the Olympic boxer Euthymus enters the story:

But Euthymus chanced to come to Temesa at the very time when the citizens were carrying out rituals of propitiation; when he learned what was happening, he wanted very much to enter the temple and see the girl. When he did see her, he first was moved to pity; then he fell in love with her. The girl swore that, if he saved her, she would marry him, so Euthymus donned his armour and waited for the coming of the daemon. He fought it and he won, and the Hero was driven out of the land; it sank under the sea and disappeared. Euthymus had a splendid wedding and the people of Temesa were freed from this daemon for ever.[176]

Elsewhere, Pausanias saw a painting of the struggle, in which the Hero was represented.

He is grotesquely black in colour, an absolutely terrifying spectacle, and he wears a wolf-skin; the lettering on the painting gives his name as Lykas (Wolf).[177]

As for Euthymus, we hear he did not die naturally but, like Kleomedes before him (see p. 144), vanished into thin air, as true heroes were wont to do.[178] This is the sort of tale beloved by anthropologists, always keen to read symbolic meaning into its details, but, just as importantly, it shows dramatically how far removed the world and the belief-systems of antiquity are from our own. It takes place before history as we know it has been dreamt of, in societies where gods and spirits are contained in everything; where the fate of those societies might be decided by the Delphic answer of an oracle and where mankind and the supernatural can, in the minds of many, mingle freely. As importantly, too, it takes place at a time when to win at Olympia was to elevate oneself above the common mass of humanity and place oneself a little closer to the divine.

Inevitably, the stories about such champions grew in the telling. In the case of one of the most famous of all boxers, Diagoras, who won his victory at Olympia in 464 BC, we can even trace his legend mushrooming. For, sixteen years later (in 448 BC), he saw his two sons take the crown in two separate events. We have three different (and increasingly extravagant) accounts of what happened next. According to Pausanias, the boys 'carried their father through the crowd, while the Greeks all pelted him with flowers and congratulated him on his sons'.[179] Plutarch develops the story. He tells how a Spartan ran up to Diagoras,

the Olympian victor, who had lived long enough to see not only his sons but the sons of his sons and daughters crowned at Olympia, and said: 'Die now, Diagoras; you cannot be a god.'[180]

But this is not the end, for later, the Roman, Aulus Gellius, embroiders the story still further. Increasing the number of Diagoras' victorious sons from two to three, he tells how

> he saw them all win victories and be crowned at Olympia on the same day. The three boys were all embracing him, garlanding their father's head with their crowns and kissing him, and all the people were congratulating him and showering him with flowers, when there in the stadium itself, in the full sight of all, amidst the hugs and kisses of his sons, he died.[181]

It was commonplace in antiquity to consider such a death, at the height of one's happiness, to be most blessed.[182] It is not difficult to see how it came to be part of Diagoras' story. The victories of his descendants were real enough, though. In Pausanias' day, the Altis bristled with their statues, and people still remembered Diagoras' daughter, the famous Pherenike, later to be called Kallipateira, the lady who had trained her son to box and had inadvertently revealed her gender as she leapt over the barrier to congratulate him when he won (see p. 68).

If boxing produced athletes who were like supermen, the next event produced the toughest of them all. This was the climax of the contact sports, the most violent and bloody of any contest staged in the Greek world: the pankration. The name means literally 'total power', and there were scarcely any rules. Even the two we know of – no biting and no gouging out the eyes – appear to have been honoured more in their breach than in their observation. As a boy, Alcibiades, an enthusiast for the sport, had famously been reprimanded for biting his opponent's hand 'like a woman'. 'No, not like a woman,' he retorted: 'Like a lion!'[183] No

56. *A judge (right) gets ready to intervene as a pankratist breaks the rules and tries to gouge out his opponent's eyes. Red-figure pottery, Athens, c.490–480 BC. Height 12.3 cm.*

doubt he took a particular interest in the pankration of 416 BC. If he did, he would be looking out particularly for one man: Androsthenes from the nearby mountains of Menailos in Arcadia. For Androsthenes had won the pankration in the last Olympic Games (420 BC) – and the word was: he could win again.

Androsthenes: the name means Man-Strength, and every strength a man might possess was channelled into the pankration. Theirs was

> a dangerous brand of wrestling. They have to endure black eyes … and learn holds by which the fallen can still win, and they must be skilful in the various arts of strangulation. They

bend ankles and twist arms and throw punches and jump on their opponents.[184]

It was visceral and brutal, a blood-spattered chaos of barbaric brawling and bare-knuckle fight, where to smash, to strangle, to subdue was to win the greatest glory, and where to unleash the greatest violence and to cause the greatest damage was to be praised by the whole of the Greek-speaking world as the greatest hero of them all. In the end, as always, there were only two. And, this year, one was Androsthenes.

If he had any time to think of anything (and he had not), as he wiped the bloody sweat from his forehead and raised his right arm for the hammer-blow, Androsthenes might have reflected on his predecessor Arrhakhion from nearby Phigalia, a city known for witches and for worshipping a black Demeter with a horse's head. For, almost a century and a half before (564 BC), Arrhakhion too had been a champion – two times the winner of the Olympic pankration. But when he came a third time to the Altis,

> his opponent, whoever he was, got a grip first and held Arrhakhion with his legs squeezed round his neck at the same time. Meanwhile, Arrhakhion dislocated a toe on his opponent's foot but was strangled and expired. At the same moment, however, Arrhakhion's opponent gave up because of the pain in his toe. The Eleans proclaimed Arrhakhion the victor and crowned his corpse.[185]

A sweet victory perhaps, but one which could be savoured by others only. As he fastened his forearm more tightly round his opponent's throat, strangling him with such deadly virtuosity, Androsthenes could spare no thought for even Theagenes, the champion from Thasos who had once beaten the great daemon-slayer Euthymus himself (see p. 148f.) in boxing, and who had excelled, too, at the pankration. From his earliest days, Theagenes seemed destined for great things:

> When he was nine years old, they say, the boy was walking home from school one day when he was attracted by a bronze statue of some god or other that stood in the market place. He hoisted it up and carried it home over his shoulder. The people were outraged at this behaviour, but an elderly citizen of some distinction would not allow them to kill the boy. Instead, he ordered him to carry the statue back from his house to the market place. The boy did so, and immediately became very famous for his strength, as what he had done was spoken about throughout Greece.[186]

This was the type of fame Androsthenes would like, as, perhaps on the ground now, he drove his knee hard into his opponent's back, at the same time pulling the man's head back by the hair. Of course, being a victor in the Games meant having enemies. Not that this would worry Androsthenes. But (on another occasion, when he was less preoccupied) he might have recalled (with a wry smile) what happened when the same Theagenes had died:

> A man who had loathed him while he lived came every night to whip the bronze statue of Theagenes as if he were assaulting Theagenes himself: the statue toppled over onto him and put an end to his impious behaviour.[186]

Divine justice, Androsthenes might have thought (though for now, perhaps, he was more intent on breaking his opponent's fingers).

And as for what happened next …

> The man's sons prosecuted the statue for murder, and the
> Thasians took the opinion of Drakon, who rules in the
> Athenian murder laws, that even inanimate objects which fall
> on a man and kill him must be taken outside the boundaries,
> and they drowned Theagenes' statue in the sea. In the course
> of time, the earth of Thasos ceased to give fruit, so they sent
> ambassadors to Delphi and the god in his oracle … replied
> to them: 'You leave great Theagenes unremembered.' They
> say that while they were in despair of how to rescue
> Theagenes' statue some fishermen let down nets into the sea
> for a catch of fish; the statue was entangled in their net and
> they brought it back to land. The Thasians dedicated it again
> where it had first stood, and they offer customary sacrifices
> to it as a god.[187]

As a god… That was something with which Androsthenes
could perhaps identify, even if the balanced stories about the
statues seemed suspiciously neat. But nothing could be allowed to
distract him now, as he concentrated hard (maybe) on trying to
dislocate an irritatingly unwilling shoulder. Not even the thought
of other pankratists to come. Had he but known it, even as
Androsthenes tightened his vice-like grip around his opponent's
bulging upper arm, rough with sand and slick with sweat and
blood, the biggest and the brawniest pankratist of all was growing
up in Thessaly in the city of Skotoussa. His name was Poulydamas,
and eight years later (408 BC), he too would come to Olympia
where he would win his match. Like Timanthes from Kleonai (see
p. 145), Poulydamas too sought to rival Heracles. Soon stories
about him would multiply: how he killed a lion with his bare

hands on Mount Olympus; how he fought an angry bull and seized its hoof and clung on tight, and how the bull, incensed, escaped him only when its hoof became detached, clasped firm in Poulydamus' close-clenched hand; or how he stopped a chariot in its tracks by clinging to the back of it – no matter how determinedly the driver whipped his horses, the vehicle would not budge …[188]

But Poulydamus' day had not yet come. Today the prize went to Androsthenes, for even now the other man had screamed that he surrendered, and the roar of the crowd was mingled with the pounding of the blood in his hard-battered head. Androsthenes had won. For the second time. He was being carried on the shoulders of his friends. A ribbon was being tied around his forehead. And his opponent, broken and bloody, was being gently carried off to nurse his awful wounds.

Androsthenes is the last of the Olympic winners of 416 BC whose name we know. But he was not the last to win. For there was still one further contest to be held: a race distinct from any other which had yet been run so far, the race by men in armour. It had been introduced a hundred years before, in 520 BC, at a time when Greek warfare was dominated by one class of fighting man: the hoplite. And what characterized the hoplite most was one key piece of equipment: his shield (or *hoplon*). Round and bevelled, sometimes simple, sometimes prodigiously ornate, the shield was perhaps a metre in diameter. The outer face of its wooden frame was encased in metal, while the inner side was furnished with one leather strap through which the warrior would pass his left arm, and a second which he grasped in his left hand. It was not only for defence. An upward jab or a sideways swipe, or a slice from the metal rim could cause unimaginable damage. To throw away the shield was the basest act of the lowest

57. *Mirror image: two runners in the hoplon-race carry shields, showing runners in identical poses to their own. Red-figure pottery, Athens, c.450 BC. Height 27.2 cm.*

coward. Spartan mothers, when their sons set out for battle, urged them to return in only one of two ways: either carrying their shield or carried on it – as a corpse. The shield personified its wearer. Many chose to invest their shields with magic talismans – mystic mythical designs to terrify the enemy. Only Alcibiades defied the trend. His shield bore a design of Eros, god of lust.[189]

There were no such designs on the twenty-five Olympic shields, all housed for safe-keeping in the Temple of Zeus, each one identical and of an equal weight, so that no athlete might be favoured. Now they had been brought out to the west end of the running track, where the athletes[190] already stood, naked as for every contest, save now for their lower legs which were encased in greaves.[191] These, like the helmets they would also wear, must have belonged to the runners themselves, as, for them to fit comfortably, they were made to measure.

The origins of the race are obscure, and possibly even in 416 BC no one quite remembered how it had begun. Ask an Elean, and he would possibly have spun the yarn that Pausanias heard some six

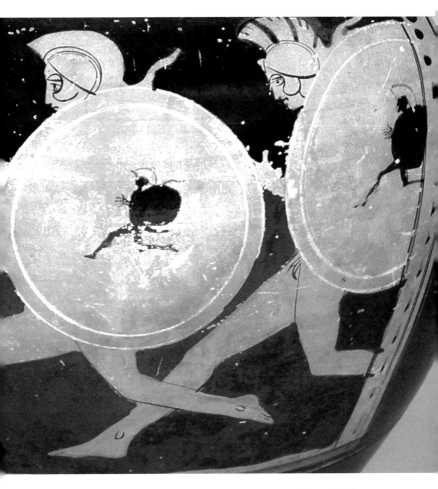

centuries later — of how, in time of war, an armed man had run into the stadium with the news that Elis had won a famous victory.[192] It is more likely it that it had its origins in military exercises.[193] Certainly, the image of the heroic warrior, naked save for helmet, shield and spear, became commonplace on vases everywhere — a representation not of real warfare, but of the

58. *Fantasy battle: a representation of the Homeric fight between Hector and Achilles imagines the two warriors dressed not in armour but for the hoplon-race. Red-figure pottery, Athens, c.490–460 BC. Height 63 cm.*

athlete-warriors of the *hoplon*-race engaged in fantasy battle.

Whatever the truth, as the spectators watched the runners fit on their heads first the felt under-cap, then the skull-encircling helmets – each one polished till it glittered in the August sun – and then pick up their shields, some of the older men among them might have recalled how, years before, Herodotus the historian, standing in the portico of Zeus' temple, had read from his account of the Battle of Marathon (490 BC, see p. 19). The Greeks, those fighting few from Athens and Plataea, were stationed on the rise above the flatlands and the sea, where the Persian army milled in all their tens of thousands. When the command came, as Herodotus himself had written:

> the Athenians advanced at a run towards the enemy, not less
> than a mile away. The Persians, seeing the attack developing
> at the double, prepared to meet it confidently enough, for it
> seemed to them suicidal madness for the Athenians to risk

an assault with so small a force – at the double, too …
They were the first Greeks, so far as I know, to charge
at a run …[194]

Marathon, he might have said, prefiguring another later battle,
had been won on the racetracks of Olympia and the other playing
fields of the Greek world. The race in armour, then, was a deadly
serious ending to a deadly serious Games. The great poet Pindar
had himself once linked the disciplines of war and sport:

whoever wins fragile fame
                from winning in games
                or fighting in battle
wins eulogies and praise
                from fellow citizens
                and countless foreigners alike
the greatest prize of all[195]

Two lengths of the running track:[196] first west to east; and then
the turning point before the shining, shimmering athlete-
warriors raced down the final strait towards the great ash altar
and the temples in the groves to Zeus and Hera; and so across the
finishing line, and for one man his victory.

It was the final struggle of the Festival, the last burst of
adrenalin, as the cheers and jeers and shouting from the now
well-trodden stadium slopes resounded from the temples and the
statues and the wooded hillsides round the valley of the Alpheios.
The Festival was nearly done. But there was still the final day, the
day when victory would be acknowledged and the victors
crowned, the day of feasting and congratulations, and, for some,
the day when last negotiations might be made. And on their

outcome might hang a struggle which would result in other struggles, more deadly by far than any played out on the Olympic sand: struggles between cities and peoples where the prize was not an olive crown but life. Or death.

CHAPTER 6

# CELEBRATING VICTORY

## DAY 5 (FULL MOON PLUS TWO)

For many of the tens of thousands gathered at Olympia, the last few days must have concentrated the mind wonderfully. Some of the traders in the tented city had made money. More, no doubt, had lost it. Only a week ago, they had felt such confidence in their gamble that they easily could clear their vast and ever-spiralling overheads – the haulage costs, the shipping costs, the costs of buying in or creating stock. Now with only one day left, it was nightmarishly clear how disastrously reckless that gamble had been.

Elsewhere and more happily, artists and artisans looking for rich patrons may have found them. Philosophers and sophists looking for impressionable young protégés, ready to part with hefty fees in return for appearing fashionably clever, may have found them, too. Young dandies looking for rich lovers to support them in their modish ways had almost certainly struck lucky – if only for a night or two. But now the magic and excitement of the Festival were drawing to a close. The smell and squalor of so many tens of thousands of increasingly unwashed men living in such close proximity, in such unsanitary conditions and in such unrelenting heat, were starting to take their toll. There may have been another day or so to go, but thoughts must now have been beginning to turn to home – and to reality.

59. *Winged Victory, the goddess to whom every contestant at the Games would have prayed for success. Bronze. Tarantum, c. 500 BC. Height 15 cm. Bequeathed by Richard Payne Knight.*

Throughout the Greek world that reality was grim. There cannot have been one man there at Olympia that year who could not sense that war was in the air. Even if they had not seen the delegates from Sicilian Segesta slipping secretly inside the silken tent, the rumours must have gone the rounds about their dealings with its resident, the man at the heart of the web of diplomatic intrigue: Alcibiades. Why were the super-rich of Ephesus and Chios and of Lesbos doing so much to win his favour? Was it that they calculated that a war in Sicily would open up new business prospects – that, if Athens won, the politician Alcibiades would be well placed to offer contracts and concessions; lucrative licenses to trade in all that island's wealth, in grain and in that most rewarding of the products of the olive: oil? What of the discussions of the Dorian states, of Sparta and of Syracuse, and of their allies the Corinthians, the Thebans and the rest? Old fault-lines were already reappearing, old power games being replayed, and nowhere was this more the case than Melos.

It is unlikely any Melian was at Olympia that year. By August 416 BC it is probable that the harbour of this arid island in the south-west Cyclades was being blockaded by a small fleet of Athenian warships, the city itself cut off, besieged. It had been irritating Athens for too long, this island-state which refused to be part of the Athenians' island empire. So the Athenian ships had been dispatched, and with them (should we be surprised?) warships from both Chios and Lesbos. Melos itself was insignificant. It was the principle that counted. In his account of the affair, written within a decade afterwards, Thucydides – himself familiar with many of the players and in August 416 BC perhaps attending the Olympic Festival – broke from the narrative convention which he had imposed upon his *History* to dramatize the talks between the two sides. One speech he gives to the Athenians contains a telling line:

Both the gods (we believe) and mankind (we know) are driven by this one unbending law of nature: wherever they can, they rule.[197]

As at Olympia, so in politics: power was everything. Not, of course, that everyone agreed. Already the more prescient in Athens could sense trouble. Writing in his cloistered study on the island of Salamis, the Athenian dramatist Euripides had already begun his prophetic *Trojan Trilogy,* in which he would explore the corrupting consequences of a long siege and a drawn-out war (see p. 187).[198]

The mass of humanity, whether in their scattered homes across the Mediterranean and Aegean seas or here at Olympia on this darkling evening, were powerless to influence the course of history. Even in so-called democracies the real power lay in the hands of the generals and politicians, moguls and rich magnates, who paid lip-service to the needs of their constituents and whose votes could readily be bought for money or for promises. For all of them, the Festival had been a forum for negotiations and discussions, for sounding out potential allies, engineering 'chance' encounters, wining, dining, cutting deals; for trying to shape the way the world would look for years to come. For them, the urgent realities of political and economic life had never been far absent from their thoughts – even here at Olympia. And this evening was their last chance to hold that crucial meeting or to strike that decisive deal.

The atmosphere on this evening, after the last of the games was done, may well have been frenetic and even somewhat desperate. It seems that there was nothing formally arranged. How people spent it was left up to them. So, as the darkness thickened and the shrill notes of the cicadas drilled deep into the gathering night, the preoccupations of the crowds, which only hours before had

60. *A judge, his cane resting beside him, prepares to tie a ribbon on the head of a particularly successful young athlete – he is wearing one ribbon already. Red-figure pottery, Athens, 485–480 BC. Diameter 30.2 cm.*

been united in the common interest of the Games, were now beginning to fragment. The panhellenic passion was already giving way to personal concerns.

But there was still one great unifying event which lay ahead of them, and as the rising sun warmed the valley and the scent of pine trees drifted from the hills to mask (at least in the imagination) the encampment's stench, the many thousands of men made ready to come together for the last time to celebrate the athlete's victories. For each of the winners this was the pinnacle of their Olympic glory: for young Nikostratos, the boy wrestler from Heraia; for Androsthenes, the pankratist from Arcadia; for Alcibiades for his great chariot win; for Exainetus of Agrigentum, whose victory in the stade-race would make his fame immortal; and for all the others whose names are not recorded. For each of them the words of the poet Bacchylides would ring true:

> Zeus, thunder-blaster,
> on the banks of the silver-flowing Alpheios
> you have answered his prayers,
> you have granted him your gift:
> enormous fame.
> Around his head you have set
> the glaucous band
> of olive leaves
> won in the shining contests
> of Pelops.[199]

So they all assembled for this one last time – all the victors and the judges, all the committee members and the Elean officials, all the ambassadors and delegates from all the cities in the wide

Greek world, and they prepared for the procession. For, just as the Festival had begun four days before with a sacrifice to Zeus of Oaths, now it would end in Zeus' presence – but not, as then, in the Bouleuterion. Today the ceremony would take place in the great temple itself, before the gold and ivory statue, where the great Olympian god, enthroned in glory, held in his hand a dancing Victory.[200]

Perhaps starting at the Prytaneum, the course that the procession was to take was thickly lined with onlookers. As they emerged into the sunlight, so the singing of the ancient hymn began, full-throated, its verses honouring the hero Heracles,[201] and as the procession passed them by, the spectators on either side threw flowers and leaves high in the air to scatter down onto the victors' heads. This was the *phyllobolia,* a confetti of petals strewn and billowing, marking the passage of the athletes east across the Altis to the temple steps and to the solemn ceremony which would unfold inside. As the crowds swarmed into the area before the temple, some pressed close to statues, others crammed around the gleaming white triangular base of the tall pillar on which stood the Victory of Paionios, the official procession slowly climbed the steps and passed between the tall bronze-plated doors into the incense-drifting temple itself.

For many of them, the sense of awe and wonder must have been almost overwhelming. There they stood in Zeus' towering presence. There they had come to receive the highest accolade of all in recognition of their victory in the most famous Games in all the world The athlete's eyes must have strayed, if only for a moment, towards the table made, like the statue, of gold and ivory[202] and brought already from its usual place in the Temple of Hera to be placed here in front of the low wall which ran round the pool of oil before the statue. For on that table lay the thirteen olive wreaths, one for each of the victors in each of that year's contests. The branches for the wreaths had been cut, perhaps that very morning, from the sacred olive tree – 'beautiful for its crowns'[203] – not by the Woodsman, but by a young boy with a golden sickle.[204]

The olive tree, from which the branches for the wreaths were cut, was the most holy of all trees in the Altis. In the earliest of days, the victors at Olympia had received an apple, not an olive wreath, as prize, but legend told how Iphitus, the king of Elis, went to Delphi to enquire how the Olympic victors should be best rewarded. The answer came:

> Iphitus, no longer give the apple's fruit as prize to the victor.
> Crown him instead with a wreath from the wild and fertile olive,
> Which is now enveloped in gossamer webs.[205]

When he returned to Delphi, Iphitus examined all the olive trees in turn and found one shrouded in dewy cobwebs. From then on from this tree the wreaths were made, and even now in 416 BC it stood – old, gnarled, surrounded by an ancient fence to mark its sanctity; one of a grove of olive trees, the so-called *Pantheon*, whose branches were cut every month and laid as offerings on all the altars throughout the Altis by the priests.

Each victor's wreath, which now lay on the table, was formed from a single branch of this tree – a ring of unending power which would link its wearer in a mystic union with the god.[206] For there was in the temple a fourteenth olive wreath, the wreath of golden leaves upon the dark-haired head of the statue of Zeus himself.

How the ceremony progressed we do not know.[207] We might assume that, after an invocation and perhaps a prayer or speech, the names of the winners were read out one by one, and one by one they walked out to the front where the chief of the Elean committee placed the olive wreath with great solemnity upon the victor's head. It was an intensely potent moment, this sacrament of crowning mankind's supreme victors in the presence of the greatest god of all. What was it like, the surge of elation each man felt? Perhaps Bacchylides, the praise-poet, had come closest to capturing the sense of exaltation when he sang of the eagle in a song of triumph, written for a victor two generations earlier:[208]

Lightning-fast on tawny wings,
      the eagle,
      confident in its immeasurable strength,
cleaves the vast unfathomable sky,
      the messenger of Zeus,
      the thunder god
      whose rule is wide,

            and all the little birds,
                  shrill-chattering,
                        scatter in terror.

The high peaked mountains cannot check him,
nor the pounding storm-waves of the tireless sea,
      but on outstretched wings
      he soars
      across the vastness of the earth,
his feathers gently ruffled in the western breeze,
      and all men see him.[209]

It must have had a dream-like quality, the hearing of one's name announced; the stepping forward and the bowing of the head; the feeling of the crown being placed; the feeling of the leaves, *those leaves,* against the skin; the stepping back; the glancing up at the great statue soaring high above; the knowing that in that moment throughout all the world one's fame had become immortal.

But for his fame truly to have become immortal, the winning athlete must have commissioned (for a considerable fee) at least one of two important works of art: a praise-song or a statue. Both were his due, and it is largely thanks to their survival that we know the names and deeds of so many of the men who triumphed

at Olympia. Pausanias saw a host of statues in the Altis dating back to 416 BC and earlier. Some were wooden, some in marble, some in bronze, each painted carefully to make them seem most lifelike; their eyes impassive, yet many with a magnetism all their own. Every type of athlete was represented: runners and wrestlers, pankratists and charioteers, but (unsurprisingly, given the Eleans strict control of the sanctuary) there were strict rules

61. *Idealized, perfect and flawless, a cavalcade of devotees rides in honour of Athene. Marble relief from the North Frieze of the Parthenon, Athens, 447–432 BC. Height 99 cm.*

about how the winners should be portrayed.

No statue could be larger than life-size – only the gods could be shown as super-human. At least in later years, it was believed that if the committee judged the statue was too big, it would be toppled over.[210] In addition, portraiture was not allowed – the statues were considered to be votive offerings to Zeus in thanks for victory, so, as befitted such a gift, the winners must be represented as idealized, as perfect, as flawless as those devotees who had been represented on the dedication to Athene in the frieze which ran around the Parthenon a generation earlier. The

62. *Victory parade: an owner walks proudly in front of his winning horse and jockey while a slave carries both an olive wreath and a (somewhat heavier) tripod. Black-figure pottery, Athens, c.540–520 BC. Height 44.5 cm.*

identity of each man was revealed in an inscription on the statue base. It gave his name, his city and the event in which he had achieved his victory, and for the most part nothing else.

It was, perhaps, the equestrian statuary which was the most impressive: horses, some with riders, others riderless, and chariots, their horses yoked and harnessed; the charioteer himself, now calm and passionless, caught up in his communion with Zeus; his reins held slackly in his hands, his robes loose, limp, his face devoid of all emotion – godlike even in its inhumanity.[211] Among the many chariot sculptures which Pausanias saw, one caught his attention, a chariot in bronze 'with a man standing in it; there are racehorses beside the chariot, one on either side, with boys mounted on the horses.'[212]

It had been set up by the tyrant, Hieron of Syracuse, the man for whom Bacchylides had sung of the soaring eagle (see p. 169), and for whom that other great praise-singer Pindar had composed as well.

Praise-singing was a vital weapon in the successful athlete's panoply, as he fought to achieve an everlasting fame, and choosing the right poet was essential. Evidence suggests that commissions were quickly made, and even that short songs were written hastily, ready to be sung at celebration feasts on this, the fifth day of the Games, with longer and more burnished praise-songs being performed often years later in the athlete's native city. Rivalry between praise-singers was intense. Pindar and Bacchylides each managed to weave into their writing veiled jibes aimed at the other. For, as well as ensuring that the memory of the athlete was everlasting, at the same time the praise-song could bestow its own immortality upon the poet. Pindar was well aware of this relationship. It is, he writes, his ability to write verses 'with godlike words for all posterity' that immortalizes the athlete,

for if a man expresses something well,
his words,
   undying,
spread,

and over all the fertile earth,
and over all the sea,
the blaze of his fine deeds,
   unquenchable,
   shall shine forever[213]

Far from the prying eyes and ears of the Elean judges, these praise-songs could take on a life of their own, weaving the achievements of the athlete into long and complex narratives, binding their victories into a shared heritage of myth and legend. Many of the lyrics which survive are almost impenetrable, as they segue from one obscure reference to another. In most, in fact, the athlete plays an almost secondary role, as the poet's fancy flies ever further into the world of folk tale. Only occasionally can we experience the reality of the Olympic contest, as when Bacchylides describes Hieron's horse Pherenike. Suddenly the fogs of florid verse roll back and we are there with the spectators in the hippodrome:

Dawn, who bathes the earth in gold,
saw Pherenike,
   chestnut-maned,
   swift-running as the wind,

---

63. 'A ray whose light shall live forever': clad in a diaphanous robe, winged Victory places an olive crown on a victor's head. Sard sealstone. Hellenic, 323–31 BC. Length 2.3 cm.

win victory
by the wide-eddying Alpheios ...

Never to this day
Has he been spattered by the dust
From hooves that have out-galloped him
    as he races
    in the contest
    to his goal;
for he dashes headlong,
    racing like the north wind,
    alert always to his rider,
winning victory for Hieron
    the hospitable,
and the cheers rise up to meet him. [214]

Such a description is unusual, for it is not the reality of the
Olympic contest which interested the poet – or, we must assume,
the victor – as much as the chance to set the contest in that other-
world of legend. For, with the placing of the olive wreath upon his
head, the process of transforming the victorious athlete into a
hero had begun.

At his homecoming he would have a hero's welcome. Three
hundred chariots and six hundred snow-white horses were
waiting on the quayside to escort Exainetus to Acragas (see p.
127), while in every other city, town or village throughout the
Greek world, parades and banquets would be held to mark their
victor's homecoming. In some towns, such was the extravagance

64. *A victorious athlete, crowned with an olive wreath and holding an olive branch in his left
hand, makes an offering at an altar. Red-figure pottery, Athens, 430–420 BC, Height 25 cm.*

with which they celebrated, a stretch of city walls would ceremoniously be breached – a special threshold for their special son to cross as he came home. Bands of musicians, troupes of dancers, showers of flowers and petals, and his fellow citizens in celebration would accompany him first into the *agora*[215] and then on to the shrine which housed the statue of their patron god.

Here, at the altar, the athlete would make sacrifice in thanks. Then he would climb the steps and, walking through the doorway, stand before the statue. In a village in Arcadia, Nikostratos, the young boy wrestler, would stand before a wooden effigy of Hera. In the mountains of Menailos, where travellers could sometimes hear the god Pan play his pipes,[216] Androsthenes would stand before a rustic Athene. And in Athens, Alcibiades, his perfumed hair cascading down in ringlets over his embroidered cloak, would stand tall in the Parthenon before the gold and ivory Athene (the work of Pheidias) and drink in its power. Then each man would remove his olive wreath and dedicate it to the god. In the evening came the banquets, praise-songs and escorting of the victorious athlete home, back to his house, in triumph.[217]

For many, this was not the end. In Athens and elsewhere the victor would be granted special seating in the theatre and free meals in the city's Prytaneum[218] for life. In Athens, too, for generations it had been the rule to reward returning Olympic winners with money: 500 drachmas, more than a hoplite soldier could expect to earn in three seasons of campaigning. It was in Sparta, though, that the returning athlete was awarded what for him would be the highest accolade of all: the right to die fighting beside his king in the front line of battle.

For now, though, all this lay ahead. As the last of the athletes, the winner of the race in armour, received his olive wreath, there was a final flurry of flowers scattered from the gallery which ran around the temple.[219] Then they all turned and filed back to the outside world, to the here-and-now of celebration, the ear-splitting shouts of acclamation, the thunderous applause.

There must have been one final ceremony, though no trace of it remains, one final sacrifice to Zeus, perhaps, made on the ashen altar. There was a banquet that night, held in a special dining room within the Prytaneum complex,[220] and for there to be meat served at that banquet there must have been a sacrifice. It is likely that it was at the close of the official Festival that this sacrifice was made – the final herding of the oxen up along the ramps and so onto the platform; the final wielding of the final axe, the final fires. Perhaps concluding speeches, too, were made, the last hymns sung. And, if for many of those gathered there this was the end, for the victors there was still a feast, the last act of the Festival, the closing of the 91st Olympiad.

No doubt there were already those who were dismantling their tents and packing up their wares, eager to be off, keen to beat the crowds, intent on getting on the roads before they became too clogged, to reach the next town before the night fell, to make it to the sea to catch an early boat.

In the hubbub of departure there were perhaps some, too, who lingered, relishing these final moments in which they could still make their mark. Perhaps even now the artist Zeuxis was still hanging round the Altis, cutting an eccentric dash. Nearly fifty now, he had appeared at Olympia clad in a flamboyant, lurid cloak onto which he had embroidered his own name in lettering of gold. An exhibitionist, no doubt, but a formidable artist nonetheless, he was in the vanguard of a movement which had perfected the technique of *trompe l'oeil*, creating paintings of grapes so realistic that birds had been seen to fly down and try to eat them. For another of his canvases, his 'Helen', he had declared that he could find no woman beautiful enough to be his model, so he had worked with several, amalgamating the most winsome elements of each of them until he produced perfection. An old man, he would die, choking with laughter, as he gazed at one of his pictures. No one, we imagine, died laughing at his gold-stitched cloak, but it did excite some mirth.[221]

With all the press of the spectators, with the heat and the unhealthy sanitation, death at Olympia was, of course, inevitable and, in the past, the Festival had seen some celebrated fatalities, especially among the elderly. Among these was Chilon. Some time shortly after 556 BC, Chilon's son won the boxing contest. Chilon, who was present, was, of course, ecstatic. He embraced his victorious son and, overcome by excitement and old age, he promptly died. An unremarkable story, and one which follows a predictable pattern (see Diagoras, p. 149f.), but the significance lies in Chilon's identity, for Chilon claimed to be the author of many of the wise sayings which have come down from antiquity – sayings like 'Know Yourself', which was considered so profound that it was carved onto the Temple of Apollo at Delphi. As befitted a Spartan, Chilon's sayings were, for the most part, laconic, and included observations such as: 'honour old age'; 'do not speak ill of the dead'; 'do not hurry too much on your way'; 'do not mock the misfortunate'; 'do not spend too much money on a wedding'; and

65. *The heart of the Altis today: the Temple of Hera is seen from nearby the site of the towering ash altar of Zeus.*

'enjoy quietness'. His death at Olympia provoked a great outpouring of emotion. Diogenes Laertius, a third century AD biographer, records:

> All those present at the Festival joined in the funeral procession in his honour. I myself have written this epigram about him:

Light-bearer Polydeuces, I give you thanks
    That Chilon's son won the green olive sprig for boxing.
If, seeing his son crowned in victory, his father died of
    happiness,
We should not grieve for him. In such a way, may death
    come to me, too.[222]

Many disputed Chilon's authorship of the advice to 'know yourself'. There were those who claimed that its author was, in fact, Thales, the polymath from the Ionian sea-port of Miletus – so it is a matter of curious coincidence that Thales, too, was said by some to have died at Olympia (in 548 BC). An outstanding philosopher and geometer, Thales believed that all things are created from water. He also wrote books on solstices and equinoxes, correctly predicting not only a solar eclipse but, one year, a particularly successful olive harvest. In fact, so certain of this was he, that he bought up all the olive presses in Miletus and made a very healthy profit. Water and sun: neatly, it was a lack of one and too much of the other that caused his death:

    Thales, the philosopher, died while watching athletic games
    from a combination of heat, thirst and frailty, for he was
    very old. This is the epitaph carved on his headstone:
    You are gazing on the tomb of Thales the polymath,
    A small tomb, but his fame is as towering as the heavens.[223]

Even this year, in 416 BC, there must have been some who journeyed to Olympia never to return. For the victorious athletes, however, attending the banquet in the Prytaneum, the reality of the masses swarming on the plain outside the Altis – packing their belongings, doing one last deal, readying themselves for the long journey home – must have seemed very distant. This may well have been a cause of some frustration for one man. For Alcibiades knew that it was often in this short time after the official Festival was over, that important political meetings would take place involving key decisions which could lead to war or peace.

Only twelve years before (428 BC) the Spartans had arranged to hold a meeting with their allies in the Temple of Zeus itself, in which they invited the islanders of Lesbos (who in 416 BC were openly enthusiastic about Alcibiades) to present their argument for why the Spartans should support them in their bid to break away from the Athenian Empire. The Lesbians' speech had ended with these words, so powerful in the context of the Festival which had just gone before and of the building in which the meeting was being held:

> We ask you to respect the hopes set on you by all the
> Greeks, and to respect Olympian Zeus, in whose temple we
> stand as suppliants. Come to the help of Mytilene. Be our
> allies, and do not desert us.[224]

Alcibiades would have remembered, too, how the Spartans had agreed; how they had voted to invade the land of Athens; how they had ordered their allies to assemble for the war; how they had 'got ready the machines to haul the warships across the Isthmus, from the Corinthian Gulf to the sea on the side of Athens, so they could launch their attack simultaneously by land and sea'.[225] In the end, the attack had not come off. But that did not lessen in any way the danger of such meetings at Olympia.

No doubt Alcibiades, detained at the official banquet in the Prytaneum, had agents everywhere who would report back

anything they heard, for there was much that might concern him.
Could someone have slipped through the tight blockade at Melos,
for example, and even now be trying to enlist Sparta's support to
come and save them? No records survive of any such meetings in
416 BC. They must have happened though – it is only that the
secrecy in which they were conducted stopped any reports of
them from leaking out.

With the victory banquet over, the members of the Elean
Olympic committee must have allowed themselves a moment (at
least) of self-congratulation. Nothing untoward had happened.
There had been no real scandal. In the days ahead the last of the
tents, even that vulgar eyesore, where Alcibiades had lorded it as
if it were his own official consulate, would be taken down and the
last stragglers would leave the valley of the Alpheios. Then there
would be time enough for the great clean-up operation to be put
in place. And so, at last, the priests would have the sanctuary to
themselves again, and the normal cycle of the rituals and
sacrifices could resume.

At some point in the next few years, they would have to turn
their minds to the next Festival, the 92nd, but for the time being
all that could wait. For now they could perhaps be grateful that
the focus of the world had shifted far away – these were uncertain
times and there were benefits in being a neutral backwater.
Perhaps they speculated what the next four years would bring.
Perhaps they knew that things must change. But no one, not even
the official seer, could possibly have predicted the seismic shifts
which lay ahead, or how, before the athletes gathered at Olympia
again, the fortunes of the greatest states in the Greek world
would change dramatically.

CHAPTER 7

# FALLOUT: HUBRIS, NEMESIS AND ALCIBIADES

416 BC – 404 BC

In the aftermath of the Olympic Festival of 416 BC, events began to move with an ever faster and more dangerous momentum. In Athens, this was in part thanks to the policy and actions of Alcibiades. But soon even he was to find that war has a tendency to pick up an impetus of its own, which, once set in train, can unravel in savagely unpredictable ways.

By late August 416 BC Alcibiades was back in Athens, his victory in the chariot race the talk of every bar and banquet; the acclamation of his fellow citizens sweet music to his ears. A praise-song from Euripides and a painting from Aglaophon dedicated on the Acropolis (see p. 90) made sure that memories of his achievements would not fade. But it was in the political arena that he most desired to shine – for his ambition was for not just fame but power.

Winter (416–415 BC) saw a flurry of activity. Precise dates are difficult to pin down, but, in the months which followed the Olympic Festival, there were developments on two major fronts. First, on Melos (the island which had been under blockade by the Athenian fleet since sometime in the summer) the endgame came when members of a faction sympathetic to Athens opened the city

gates one night and let in the besieging army. With no other
option, the Melians surrendered unconditionally. The response
was brutal. Under orders from the Democratic Assembly urged
on by Alcibiades, the victorious Athenians butchered all the men
of military age and over. The women and children they sold into
slavery. One of the women was said to have been bought by
Alcibiades himself; rumour said he fathered a son by her.[226]

With the situation in Melos resolved, Athens and Alcibiades could
fix their sights further afield on an altogether more enticing and
potentially more lucrative target: Sicily. In the months after the
Olympic Festival, (encouraged, perhaps by their talks in Alcibiades'
tent) representatives from Segesta had come to Athens urging the
Assembly to send a military force to help them in their spat with
the neighbouring city of Selinus. It was the perfect pretext for a
major war. As the historian Thucydides observed:

> The truth was that the Athenians' objective was to take
> possession of the whole island, while wanting at the same
> time to present the operation in the light of an ethical policy
> to assist their own people and their newly acquired allies.[227]

The loudest of the voices raised in support of the Segestan
delegation was that of Alcibiades. Soon a 'fact-finding mission'
was dispatched to Sicily, and in early Spring (415 BC) it reported
back in favour of the war. Money, it assured the Athenians, would
be readily forthcoming: the Segestans had already provided
enough to pay for sixty warships for a month, and more, much
more, was in their treasury. Encouraged by such reports (which
only later proved to be greatly exaggerated), their passion
enflamed by Alcibiades' rhetoric, the Athenian Democratic
Assembly voted for war.

Only a few voices were raised in dissent. Among these was Nikias, the general of many years' experience, who had helped to draft the peace treaty in 421 BC and had worked so hard to cement relations with the Spartans, only to see his efforts undermined by Alcibiades (see p. 36). Reminding the Assembly of how it had sent an expedition to Sicily some years before with inconclusive results (427 BC), he urged caution.

At the same time, in the Theatre of Dionysus, Euripides, the playwright who had recently penned the praise-song for Alcibiades' victory in the Olympic chariot race, presented his *Trojan Trilogy* – a cycle of three tragedies which explored the corrosive effects of war upon both victors and vanquished alike. In the light of recent events at Melos, it was particularly penetrating. The last play in the cycle, *Trojan Women,* saw a city sacked, its menfolk slaughtered and its women sold into slavery. But running through its drama was a stark reminder that, because of their *hubris*[228] and impiety, the victors would themselves soon be destroyed.[229] Its message could not have been more timely. As Herodotus had read out from his *Histories*, standing in the portico of Zeus' temple at Olympia only a few years before, it reminded its audience that in an ideal world no one is so foolish that he will choose war over peace – for in peace, sons bury their fathers; in war fathers bury their sons.[230]

The question of whether to send the fleet to Sicily fractured Athenian opinion. The choice of Alcibiades to lead it deepened the divide. Older, wiser heads mistrusted his ardour, suspecting him of having ambitions to conquer not only the whole of Sicily but Carthage, too – and all to enhance his personal wealth and reputation.[231] And Alcibiades' riposte? He cited in evidence for his selfless support of the Athenian cause his performance at Olympia those few short months before, which had been designed, he said, merely to enhance his city's prestige:

Beforehand, they had thought optimistically that Athens had
been worn down by the war, but thanks to me and my
brilliance at the Olympic Festival, they have come to consider
our city to be even greater than it really is. For I entered seven
chariots – something no private individual had ever done before
– and I took first, second and fourth place,[232] and I made sure
that everything was done in a way which was worthy of my
victory. Achievements such as these always brings honour, but
impressed in the memory they leave the imprint of power.[233]

It was said that no one (except Socrates) could resist Alcibiades'
sexual allure;[234] now, it seemed, few in the Assembly could resist
his political charisma. So, at midsummer of that year (415 BC) the
people of Athens thronged the quayside at Piraeus to watch the
sailing of a great armada – its warships richly decorated, its troops
all eager for the fight, and at its head the ardent Alcibiades, a
general called Lamachus and his reluctant colleague Nikias.

> With the crews and the equipment all on board the ships, a
> trumpet rang out to proclaim silence. Then the usual prayers for
> a good voyage were offered up, not by each ship separately but
> by all together, led by the herald. Wine was poured into great
> mixing bowls, and the entire army, both officers and men, made
> offerings from cups of gold and silver.[235] On the shore, too, the
> crowd of citizens and all the others who had come to wish them
> well joined in their prayers. The army sang the victory hymn to
> Apollo, and when the offerings had been completed, they put
> out to sea. They sailed out of harbour in a column, then they
> raced against each other all the way to Aegina.[236]

Such were the celebrations that it must have seemed as though the mission had already been accomplished. Such was the *hubris* of Athens and of Alcibiades. But in the beliefs of the Greek world, man's *hubris* led to the anger of the gods, their *phthonos,* which led, in turn, to punishment and retribution: *nemesis.* The first blow fell almost immediately. Its target was Alcibiades.

In the days leading up to the sailing of the fleet, an act of unimaginable sacrilege had rocked the city. Standing stiffly before the door of every house throughout Athens was a statue of Hermes. With its bearded face and prominent phallus each of these *herms*, as they were called, was designed to ward off evil. Now, with the great armada ready for the off, Athenians had awoken to find that most of these stone or terracotta statues had

66. *As a Greek warship is rowed at speed, its deadly 'beak', with which it could ram enemy vessels, emerges from beneath the waves. Black-figure pottery, Athens, 520–500 BC. Diameter 20.3 cm.*

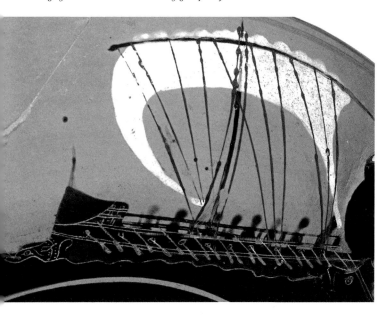

been vandalized, the streets a crunch of desecrated fragments. Fingers of blame pointed everywhere, but it was not long before Alcibiades' enemies, led by Andocides (see p. 110f.) were accusing him.[237] To back up their claims of his impiety, they produced witnesses that he had mocked the most solemn rituals of all, the Eleusinian Mysteries, in which initiates were shown the secrets of death and resurrection. The Athenian Assembly, as quick to hate as it was to love, sent out the state ship to arrest Alcibiades and bring him back for trial. Had both parts of the mission been successful, things might have turned out differently, but, as it was, Alcibiades neatly escaped his warders in the south of Italy and promptly disappeared.

The next time he was heard of he was in Sparta with the enemy. Such was his audacity and confidence, such was his desire for influence and power, that Alcibiades had turned his back on Athens and her citizens (for whose glory alone, or so he had so recently claimed, he had entered his seven chariots at Olympia) and turned traitor. Now he was more Spartan than the Spartans. Gone were his perfumed curls, his trailing silks, his louche Athenian ways. Now his hair was wild and matted; he was eating

67. *Even in modern Athens, the Acropolis dominates the skyline. In 416 BC much of the land now covered by houses was agricultural land and olive groves.*

nothing but black broth; he was taking daily plunges in the icy waters of the eddying Eurotas in the shadow of the jagged snow-toothed mountains of Taygetus.[238] He was associating with the most powerful men in Sparta, including one of the two kings[239] and the royal families. His power-base now included members of the governing elite, the ephors.[240] Moreover, he was using his extraordinary powers of political persuasion to deliver devastatingly astute advice to Sparta on how best to defeat Athens. Painting an exaggerated picture[241] of Athenian ambitions in the West, which represented them as having designs not only on Sicily and Carthage but, with the help of Spanish mercenaries, on Italy as well, he persuaded Sparta to send out a task-force of its own to Sicily to fight them. Just as catastrophically for his native city, he advised the Spartans to capture and permanently occupy a fortress on Athenian soil, from which it could launch lightning raids and so wear Athens down.[242]

68. A 'herm' type statue, similar to those, which his enemies accused Alcibiades of smashing on the eve of the Sicilian expedition. Marble, Roman, c.AD 150–170. Height 152.4 cm.

How Alcibiades greeted the news of his rival Nikias' death in Sicily or Athens' grim defeat, or the reports of how those of her soldiers who survived were dying slowly in the horrors of a concentration camp in the stone-quarries at Syracuse, we do not know. Nor do we know what his ambitions were, now that he realized the tide had turned and for the first time in so many years there was a real possibility that Athens might be defeated. For soon, in Sicily, much of Athens' fleet (on which she relied to control the seas) had been destroyed, and a large part of her army killed. Moreover, she was running dangerously short of money.

Yet none of this could stop the rolling cycles of the panhellenic festivals. In 412 BC, the 92nd Olympiad went on as usual quite unaffected by the turmoil boiling everywhere throughout the Greek-speaking world. As usual, the many thousands poured into the valley of the Alpheios to pitch their tents; the athletes wound their way in their procession through the flax fields and along the sacred route from Elis to Olympia; the oaths were made before the awe-inspiring statue in the Bouleuterion; the races run and victory in all the contests vied for; another hundred oxen fell to their knees, sacrificed on Zeus' ashen altar; another thirteen olive crowns were laid out on the same low table in Zeus' temple. And one of the crowns was placed, as it had been in the last festival, on the head of the runner from Acragas, Exainetus.

We have no record of political discussions held or plans hatched or deals made. But we do know that by now many of Athens' key allies were considering defecting – including Chios, the strategically important island state which had so openly courted Alcibiades at the Olympic Festival of 416 BC. Did Alcibiades have a hand in this? Did he have the gall to attend the Games of 412 BC? There is no evidence either way. But it is likely Olympia saw leading men of Chios locked in conversation with the Spartans or their allies. And soon the first moves would be made to prize the island from her alliance with Athens. They failed, but why they failed reveals much about the role of athletic festivals as a forum for summit meetings and political espionage. Thucydides explains:

> They were desperate to put out to sea, but the Corinthians were unwilling to sail with them until they had celebrated the Isthmian Festival, which was being held at that time … The Athenian delegation was present at the Festival (it had been officially invited), and there they formed a clearer picture of what what was going on vis-à-vis the Chians. As a result, when they returned to Athens, they immediately took measures to prevent the Corinthian fleet from sailing.[243]

But it was clear that it was only a matter of time before Athens' allies in the Eastern Mediterranean began to peel away, and, as a favour to his new-found Spartan friends, Alcibiades offered to help sow the seeds of rebellion among them, and chiefly among the cities whose allegiance to him personally he had so conspicuously advertised a few years earlier at Olympia: Chios, Lesbos and the powerful cities of the rich Ionian coast. And so, with a few Spartan ships, he sailed east on his mission.

It was the ultimate perversion of the Olympic ideal. For in the

Games, the aim had been to win, but not for oneself merely, for one's city. This was the ideal which Alcibiades had claimed to follow when he boasted to his fellow citizens that it really was for them that he had entered his seven chariots at the Games. Now, however, the true reality was starkly clear. If a choice had to be made, as now apparently it did, what mattered most for Alcibiades was not his city but himself; what mattered most to him was winning.

But even now, as his star seemed to shine so brightly back in Sparta, his hopes were dashed once more, and once more he was forced to run. The cause again was jealousy – and this time it was not just political. This time it was sexual, too. Although one of the two kings had supported Alcibiades, the other, Agis II, was less enthusiastic. Now, with Alcibiades in Ionia and his charismatic personality no longer dominating Sparta, a more pragmatic view of him took hold. Opinion began to shift against him. But what made King Agis particularly hostile was a calculation concerning the recent birth of his son. For it dawned on him that, because he had been keeping himself ritually pure in the wake of a recent earthquake and had not slept with his wife for well over ten months before the child was born, he could not be the father. When he discovered that his wife was secretly calling the boy 'Alcibiades', the truth became all too distressingly clear. It was a slight no Spartan could endure. The death squads were sent out to track down Alcibiades and kill him. They failed, but the episode had one unlikely sequel. For it was the cuckolded King Agis' brother Agesilaus who later arranged for their sister Kynisca to enter her chariot at the Olympic Games of 396 BC (see p. 92) to demonstrate that winning in that race (as Alcibiades had so spectacularly done in 416 BC) was a proof not of manliness, but simply of wealth.

With the assassins tracking him, not just Athens but Sparta now baying for his blood, and all the panhellenic world against him,

Alcibiades sought sanctuary in the one place left where he might just be welcome: Persia. Ever since the Greeks had defeated Xerxes and his army at Salamis and Plataea (see p. 21) and wrested back control of the Greek cities of the eastern Mediterranean coastline, the Persians had made a public show of keeping their distance. But they still retained a healthy interest in Greek affairs. Now, in return for Persian protection, Alcibiades gave some valuable advice. Both Athens and Sparta were running out of money. If Persia helped prolong the war by supporting first one side and then the next, the Greeks would (over time) exhaust themselves. And an exhausted fractured Greece could be defeated by the might of Persia. This was the ultimate betrayal – to sell not just one's city but one's whole people to the bitterest of all their enemies. And yet, in Persian palaces, with no apparent twinge of conscience, Alcibiades lorded it with 'pomp and lavishness'.[244]

In Athens, there were those who looked on the renewed Persian threat with justifiable nervousness. In 411 BC, the comic dramatist Aristophanes staged his well-known play *Lysistrata,* in which he urged his fellow citizens to come to terms with the Spartans. Although in reality such an option was unlikely, Aristophanes used the play to make a serious political point. Addressing an assembly of the women of Greece, the play's heroine Lysistrata brilliantly sets out the reality of the situation:

> You all ... share one country and one history, one family, all of you, all Greeks, all worshipping as one, competing all as one in the Olympic Games, with all of your achievements, Delphi and Thermopylae, art, architecture, literature, this special, wonderful, so fragile glory that is Greece – our enemies [i.e. the Persians] are arming themselves even as we speak, and what do you do? Slaughter Greek men, sack Greek cities.[245]

69. *No longer sport: two hoplites clash shields and brandish spears (now lost). In reality, the warriors' helmets would cover their faces, but the artist wants to reveal this fighter's identity. Marble, Turkey, c.400 BC. Length 132 cm.*

When the next Olympics came round, though, (in 408 BC) all this had changed again. By the time Eubatas, the runner from Cyrene on the sparkling coast of Libya, raced over the finishing line to win the stade race, and Poulydamas, the strapping pankratist from Thessaly (see p. 154), beat his opponents into pulpy submission, and Euagoras from Elis won the newly instituted two-horse chariot race, so that a fourteenth olive wreath now lay upon the victors' table, the kaleidoscopic pattern of the Greek world had lurched into a new configuration.

Alcibiades had not been long in Persia before he was making overtures to the Athenian admirals and generals sent out to staunch the haemorrhage of allies, offering to influence the Persians into supporting Athens in the war with Sparta (411 BC). Eventually, and almost unbelievably given what they knew of him, the Athenians agreed, and for as many as four years (411– 407 BC) Alcibiades led the troops of Athens into battle and to victory, struggling to keep open the vital trade route through the Dardanelles (the straits connecting the Aegean to the Black Sea) on which they depended for their corn supplies. It was

here he could be found in the summer of 408 BC, when far off the
festival was being celebrated at Olympia. The next year (407 BC),
he sailed back to Athens and what he might have hoped would be
a hero's welcome. But as luck would have it, his ship arrived on the
most ill-omened day of the Athenian calendar, a day on which a

particularly sacred and ancient wooden statue of Athene was removed from its shrine and taken to the sea to be ritually washed. The timing was inauspicious, an omen for the future, not only for Alcibiades and for Athens, but ultimately for the free Greek world.

For perhaps a year, Alcibiades enjoyed extraordinary power at Athens. All of the charges which had been laid against him back in 415 BC were dropped, his confiscated property returned, and he was given the unprecedented post of supreme command of the armed forces. If he had ever entertained hopes of becoming the sole ruler of his city and her empire, this was as close to seeing them realized as he would ever come. For a few brief months, he had reached the pinnacle of his ambitions. Soon, once again, the kaleidoscope would twist, and its pattern would break unrecognizably. The turning point came just off the coast near Ephesus, the city, which at Olympia ten years before, had furnished Alcibiades with his tent. Thanks, in no small part to Alcibiades' own machinations earlier, Ephesus was now on the side of the Spartans. Now, he had come to win it back for Athens. But his plans were thwarted. In his absence, Alcibiades' ships joined battle with the Spartan fleet and in the crush and crash, the splintering of hulls and shattering of oars, the Athenians were defeated (406 BC). Innocent for once of any wrongdoing, Alcibiades was nonetheless blamed for the debacle and summoned home. Of course, he did not go. Once again, he was on the run.

If *Nemesis*, the grim goddess of retribution, were really stalking Alcibiades and Athens, she could not have arranged her plot more neatly. The place which Alcibiades chose as his refuge turned out to be the scene of one of the last acts of the long drawn-out war between Athens and Sparta: the Chersonese, the bow-like spit of low-lying land which flanks the north-west passage out of the Aegean to the Dardanelles. It was here that, in his days commanding the Athenian fleet, Alcibiades had acquired estates and castles and it was to their fastnesses that he now made his way. Here in his private fiefdom with his private army and his private wealth, he lived in isolation from the warring world he had helped create. Until news came to him of Athens' folly.

The Athenian fleet was in the Dardanelles. So was the Spartan. But the Athenians had chosen a bad position for their base – a noxious beach, a sluggish creek, and with a name to match it: Aigospotamoi, 'Goat Rivers'. Alcibiades foresaw dire consequences. So he rode into their camp on horseback and sought out their generals.

> He told them that they had chosen a bad place to anchor: it had no harbour and no town nearby, so instead they had to bring in their supplies from Sestos. Moreover, they were turning a blind eye to the fact that, whenever they put in to shore, their crews were wandering off all over the place, wherever they wanted, while lying at anchor opposite them was a well-drilled army, trained to obey in silence any order that their commander gave.[246]

Of course, the generals paid no attention. Who was Alcibiades now to lecture them? So they stayed where they were for the moment, and when they did do battle with the Spartans, they were defeated. 3,000 Athenian prisoners were taken. All were slaughtered. Without a navy, and with the trade route now in enemy hands, Athens could not survive for long. The following year in 404 BC, even as preparations were being made in Elis for the 94th Olympiad, a starving Athens surrendered to her Spartan enemy. She was in no position to make terms. Eleven years before (415 BC), an arrogant Athenian Assembly had voted to put the male citizens of Melos to the sword and to drag the women and the children off to slavery (see p. 186). Now Athens could expect the same fate at the Spartans' hands. But it did not come. Instead, the Spartans dismantled the defences and the long walls linking Athens to the sea, installed a government, and spared them. In victory, the fiercest fighting force in Greece had shown a tender clemency.

However, there was still one man they could not forgive, and he was on the move once more. Reports came that he was in Phrygia. Now the Spartans set out to settle one last score. Accompanied by a small band of Phrygian soldiers, they found Alcibiades in a village in the mountains, living with a courtesan, Timandra.

> The men who had been sent to kill him, did not dare enter the house. Instead, they surrounded it and set it on fire. When Alcibiades realized what was happening, he gathered up all the clothes and bedding that he could and threw them on top of the flames. Then he wrapped his tunic round his left arm, grasped his short sword in his right, and ran out, untouched by the fire before the flames could catch hold of his clothing. At the very sight of him the Phrygians

70. *Coin of Philip II of Macedon commemorating victory in the Games. Silver, Macedonia, c.340–315 BC. Diameter 25 mm; weight 14 g.*

scattered. There was not one man who held his ground or fought him at close quarters; no, they all stood back and, with their javelins and arrows, they shot him dead.[247]

There was another version of his death, which did not involve the Spartans at all:

> He had seduced a girl from a prominent family, and had her with him; the girl's brothers were angered at his arrogant behaviour and one night set fire to the house where Alcibiades was staying. They shot him down, as I said above, when he ran out through the flames.[248]

In life, Alcibiades had possessed a shield on which he had placed a device showing Eros, god of lust, who aims his arrows at men's hearts (see p. 156). Now lust and *Nemesis* had brought him to the cottage in the wilderness, and the blazing arrows which were fired were aimed to kill him. Like the story of Theagenes the boxer and the statue (see p. 152f.) and like so many more tales from Greece, the life of Alcibiades has a neat and balanced ending. It seems almost too perfect, and yet it might also be true.

In life Alcibiades had brought his city down; in death he brought down his friends. It was in large part because of his well-publicized association with Alcibiades (as well as for his own unorthodox religious views) that Socrates was put on trial in Athens in 399 BC. One of the charges laid against him was 'corrupting the city's youth' (with special reference, no doubt, to Alcibiades). The other was impiety. The golden age of Athens, home to so many artists and philosophers, so many scientists and poets, so many radical enquiring minds, was over. And it was the maverick Alcibiades who had hastened its demise.

To say that the end of Athens had its beginnings in the Olympic Festival of 416 BC is too simplistic. Yet, it was here, on the eve of the disastrously hubristic Sicilian campaign, that Alcibiades, the city's favourite son, had behaved with such reckless abandon and with unrestrained extravagance. What should have been – indeed, what had been until then – a festival which celebrated everything that united the Greek world, had been hijacked and used by one man, Alcibiades, to promote his own ambitions. It was, in many ways, the end of one world and the birth of another.

Only eight years later (408 BC), the Victors' Lists contain the name, Archelaos, as winner of the four-horse chariot race. Beside it is his country, the first time that it has appeared here at Olympia, but not the last. For Archelaos, son of King Perdikkas, had come from Macedonia. It was a land, which in the century to follow would produce another victor, Philip, who would not only win the chariot race at three successive Olympic Festivals (356 BC, 352 BC and 348 BC), but whose son would deal the death blow to the freedom of Greek states and herald a future in which it would no longer be self-ruling cities who competed at Olympia, but subject members of a wider empire.

Philip's son never came to the Olympic Games, although he travelled widely. His influence was felt there nonetheless. His name, of course, was Alexander, and he belonged to a new age.

71. *Herald of a new age: Coin picturing Alexander the Great, whose campaigns would change the face of the Greek world forever. Silver. Lampascus, c.305–281 BC. Weight 17.2 g.*

# THE NEXT 877 YEARS, A BRIEF HISTORY

416 BC – AD 462

The boy athletes who won crowns at the Olympic Festival of 416 BC may never have been victors in their adult lives (see p. 65), but, by the time that they were old and reminiscing, they could complain with utter truthfulness that the Games were not what they used to be. So many things had contributed to change. Some were minor, some more major, but by the early years of the fourth century BC, the Games had become more secular.

Politics had played its part. The Greek world at the end of the Peloponnesian War (404 BC) was a different place to what it had been even twelve years earlier, and, in the century which followed, it would change beyond all recognition. In 400 BC, the Spartans, still smarting from being excluded from the Games twenty years previously (see p. 33), took their revenge, launching an attack on Elis and forcing the city to surrender on humiliating terms. Naked politics and war were nudging closer to Olympia. A generation later, in 364 BC, war encroached even into the Altis itself when an Elean army, furious because their ancient enemy from Pisa (see p. 18) had wrested control of the Festival from them the year before, launched an attack upon the sanctuary during the Games. The historian Xenophon, who lived nearby, describes the outrage:

They had already finished the equestrian events and those events of the pentathlon which are held in the stadium. The athletes who had come through to the wrestling were no longer in the stadium but in the area between the racecourse and the altar. The men of Elis, fully armed, had by now reached the sacred precinct. So the Pisan side, without advancing, fell into formation by the river Kladeos (which flows past the Altis and into the Alpheios). With them as allies were about two thousand hoplites from Argos and four hundred Athenian horsemen. They all made sacrifice and then advanced …

They pursued the enemy as far as the area near the Bouleuterion … The Eleans fought bravely and pushed forward towards the altar, all the while being pelted with missiles from the roofs of the stoas and the Bouleuterion and the great Temple of Zeus. Some of their men were killed … and they returned to camp.

But the Pisans were apprehensive about what would happen the next day, so they worked through the night dismantling the encampment[249] and building defences. When the Eleans returned in the morning they saw how strong the defences were, with many men positioned on the temple roofs, so they withdrew to their own city.[250]

72. *The row of bases for zanes statues leads down to the arched entrance to the new*
*stadium, relocated in the fourth century* BC.

Years later, Pausanias heard from his guide at Olympia that

> in his lifetime the roof of the Temple of Hera had required
> repair, and in the space between the ornamented ceiling and
> the tiles, the Eleans who were working on it found the corpse
> of a badly wounded hoplite. He must have fought in the battle
> … weak from his wounds, he must have crawled into this space
> and died. Now dead, his body was protected from the summer
> heat and winter frost, because it was so well sheltered.[251]

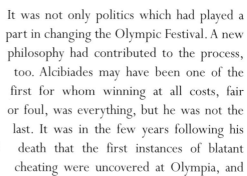

73. *An aberration? Athletes in 416 BC would have found the introduction of a contest for trumpeters and heralds (less than a century later) bizarre. Bronze, Campania, 480–460 BC. Height 15.2 cm. Bequeathed by Sir William Temple.*

It was not only politics which had played a part in changing the Olympic Festival. A new philosophy had contributed to the process, too. Alcibiades may have been one of the first for whom winning at all costs, fair or foul, was everything, but he was not the last. It was in the few years following his death that the first instances of blatant cheating were uncovered at Olympia, and the so-called Zanes statues were erected (388 BC, see p. 59 and figs 21 and 72). But more that anything, an ambitious building programme at Olympia had changed the nature of the site, physically separating the racecourse and the hippodrome from the Altis, its religious heart. The sacred had been removed from the secular. The Games had lost their soul.

It is perhaps not a coincidence that it was even as the chariot teams of Philip, King of Macedon, were thundering to victory in the roaring hippodrome that these changes were taking place. The first change was also the most significant. The position of stadium was moved. For four hundred years the runners in the foot-races had raced to victory in the shadow of the temple and ash-altar of Zeus. Now the stadium was relocated almost a hundred metres to the east.[252] The reason was pragmatic. Greater numbers of spectators needed an increased capacity, and to allow for this the track (for the first time) became enclosed, surrounded on four sides by an earth embankment. The significance of this was huge. Because the embankment on the narrow western side – the side of the track where the winning line was crossed – was well over five metres high, the runners could not see beyond it. The Altis with its temples and its shrines, with the Pelopion and with the sacred ashen altar, was completely hidden. The races, even the stade-race whose winner gave his name to each Olympic cycle of four years, had been removed forever from the sanctuary.

Now that the stadium was physically separated from the sacred area, there was no reason why the hippodrome should not be, too. In the next few years a Colonnade was built along the eastern edge of the Altis, its southern end extending so far that the charioteers, whipping their horses down the final straight, could not see (even if they had the time to look) the Temple of Zeus with its depiction of the preparations of Pelops for his chariot race glinting on the pediment. In time, the Eastern Colonnade became the venue for two newly instituted contests, contests which the athletes of the Olympic Festival's early years, bent as they were on physical prowess and heroic glory, would have found bizarre: the contests for trumpeters and heralds.[253] And the reason why the Colonnade became the venue for these clamorous contests? It echoed. It caused a sound to be repeated more than seven times.[254] What aberration on the part of the Elean authorities could possibly have let them think that such contests were a worthy addition to the ancient Games? The shades of Milo and

74. *The Philippeion today: an elegant round temple which housed statues not of gods but of the Macedonian royal family, it spoke of a chilling new world order.*

Euthymos, not to mention Heracles and Pelops, must have shaken their spectral heads in disbelief.

But this was not to be the end of such new horrors, not by a long shot. Perhaps the building of a hotel complex (330–320 BC) just outside the Altis to the south could be excused. Funded at his own expense by one, Leonidas of Naxos (a developer with a sound eye for profit), it occupied an area some eighty metres square[255] between the river Alpheios and the workshop where, only a hundred years before Pheidias had crafted his great statue of Zeus. Laid out around a central courtyard, planted with fragrant shrubs and splashing with fountains, the Leonidaion (as it inevitably was called) consisted of a warren of small rooms for guest accommodation, together with one larger hall or lobby. Now anyone with money and the foresight to book well ahead could avoid the crush and squalor of the tents and enjoy the Games in luxury.

No, it was another building, put up at the same time (just after 338 BC), which chillingly spelt out both to Olympia and to the Greek world the harsh realities of the new order. This time, it was in the Altis itself, just to west of the Temple of Hera (below whose roof the corpse of the dead soldier had already lain forgotten for

a quarter of a century and would remain for more than another four hundred years). The new building was a *tholos*, a round temple, deceptive in its elegance, a so-called votive offering from Philip, King of Macedon. What made it sinister was not its architecture (it was beautiful), or even its position (the Altis, after all, was thick with votive offerings). What made it sinister was that it housed not a victory statue (to which Philip, having won

the chariot race, was
entitled) but a whole tribe
of statues – statues, in fact, of
the entire royal family of
Macedon, made not from bronze or
marble but in gold and ivory – like the
statue of Zeus. As if they, too, were gods. And the timing of its
building could not have been more telling. It was begun after
Philip's victory in battle at Chaironeia, a battle in which his
invading Macedonian army had defeated the armies of the free
Greek states. In other words, the *tholos* was an offering in thanks
not for a victory in a chariot race but for the enslavement of the
whole of Greece. Olympia now had a new master and a new god;
and that god was a living man.

With the rise of Macedon and the rule of first Philip, and then
Alexander, and all the litany of his successors, the Greek world
changed forever, and with it the whole nature of the Games. Now
that much of the Greek-speaking world was subject to an empire,
the significance of its scattered cities coming together at the
Games was lessened. Athletics itself took on a new role.
Professional athletes toured an ever-widening circuit. Olympia
was still the pinnacle, but the religious aspect of the Festival was
less and less important. In time, another empire annexed Greece,
an empire, whose people, insofar as they did not speak Greek,

were technically barbarians: the Romans.

The ability to speak Greek had once been a prerequisite for coming to Olympia and entering the Games. Now, at a stroke, that rule was waived. Indeed, another precondition was waived, too, the rule forbidding any man whose hands were stained with sacrilege or blood-guilt from participating in the Festival. Eight years before the Roman Emperor Nero graced the Olympic Games with his presence (in AD 67), he had engineered his mother's murder. Now at Olympia he erected a triumphal arch in his own honour and commissioned a sumptuous villa for his comfort near the hippodrome, a short palanquin-ride from the Bouleuterion. How the mother-slayer felt as he took the oath before the awe-inspiring statue of Zeus, we can only imagine. In all likelihood, he was unfazed. Certainly, his subsequent performance in the chariot race did not throw him (even if his horses did):

> At Olympia he drove a ten-horse chariot team. He fell
> from his chariot and was helped back in, but he could not
> continue and gave up before the end of the race. Even so
> he received the victor's crown.[256]

Of course he did. By now there was nothing, even at Olympia, which was not subject to the power of Rome. In fact, much of Olympia had been transferred to Rome: many of the victors' statues which had graced the Altis in the days when it was free had been prized from their plinths and shipped across the seas to Italy. Even the celebrated statue of Hermes by Praxiteles had been sacrilegiously removed from the Temple of Hera. A saccharine-sweet copy had replaced it.[257]

Even the power of Rome was undermined, however. Two new and unforeseen movements were responsible. The first was the

mass migration of tribesmen from beyond the Empire's eastern
borders. In AD 267, the peoples of the Heruli, originally from the
icy Sea of Azov in the south of Russia, swept west, bursting
through the Bosphorus and fanning out to sack not only the cities
of Ionia and the Aegean sea-board of Asia Minor, but of Greece.
Athens, Corinth, Argos, Sparta: all fell to the Heruli. Perhaps
they tried to sack Olympia, too. A defensive wall was certainly
thrown up in haste around Altis. In time, the Heruli were
defeated, and for another century or so the Festival clung on. At
last, another wave of eastern immigrants moved into Greece,
plundering cities, leaving a trail of havoc in their path (AD 395–7).
These were the Visigoths, and under their leader Alaric they
would soon sack Rome itself (AD 410).[258] But even before they
pitched their tents on the banks of the Alpheios, where once the
festival-goers had pitched theirs, much of the glory which had
been Olympia had disappeared.

Many of the buildings were in disrepair and most of the statues
gone. Even the great statue of Zeus itself was no longer in his
temple. As long before as the first century AD, the despotic
emperor Caligula had tried to ship it off to Rome, but, as his
workmen strained to move it, the structure shifted and unearthly
groans were heard from deep within it, which caused everyone to
flee.[259] A later attempt (c. AD 390), in the years immediately
preceding Alaric's invasion, had been successful, and by the time
the Visigoth reached Olympia, the statue of Zeus was safe in
Constantinople, in a patrician's palace.[260]

By then, its power had been extinguished, for, in AD 391, the
emperor Theodosius I had outlawed the worship of not only Zeus

76. *Christ enthroned: the iconographers of Constantinople may have taken their inspiration
from Pheidias' statue of Olympian Zeus.*

but all the pagan gods. The Roman world had become officially Christian. It was a transformation which not even Olympia could resist and by AD 425 the last Games of all had taken place. A year later, the second Theodosius ordered the destruction of the temples. Worship did still take place, though, at Olympia. The workshop of Pheidias, where he had created his great masterpiece, the statue of Zeus (a wonder of the pagan world), was consecrated as a church. At mass, the faithful drank there from the sacred chalice, little knowing that Pheidias' own cup was buried in the soil beneath their feet (see p. 26). But by now the Altis was in ruins. The new religion had seen to that. Earthquakes (AD 522 and 551) and the river Alpheios, which changed its course and silted up the site, soon did the rest, and in time even the location of Olympia itself had been forgotten.

Yet this was not entirely the end. Although it was destroyed by fire in AD 462, Pheidias' statue of Zeus had excited a great interest in Constantinople. The features of its face especially had enthralled all who saw it. As it had done almost nine hundred years before, it made its viewers feel a sense of awe – that they had come into the presence of pure molten power. And, for Christians, that could mean only one thing: it was a true likeness of the face of God Himself. So, fired with divine inspiration, the iconographers rushed back to their studios on the banks of the Bosphorus to create their images of the new Christian God. And the face they gave their new God was the face of Zeus.

# TIMELINE

Events in *italics* represent approximate dates

| Year BC | Events at Olympia | Events in the Panhellenic World |
|---------|-------------------|--------------------------------|
| 776 | First Olympic Games<br>First stade race | |
| 753 | | *Foundation of Rome* |
| 750 | | *Spread of Greek colonies east and west* |
| 724 | First *diaulos* race | *Homer's* Odyssey *and* Iliad *written* |
| 720 | First *dolikhos* race<br>First time competitors are naked | *Hesiod's* Theogony *and* Works *written* |
| 708 | First pentathlon and wrestling | |
| 700 | *Temple of Hera built* | |
| 688 | First boxing | |
| 680 | First four-horse chariot race | |
| 648 | First pankration and horse race | *Rise of the Tyrants* |
| 632 | First boys' foot-race and wrestling | |
| 616 | First boys' boxing | |
| 564 | Arrhakhion killed in pankration | |
| 556 | *Chilon dies at Olympia* | |
| 505 | | *Democracy established in Athens* |
| 500 | *First stadium built* | |
| 548 | *Thales dies (? at Olympia)* | |
| 520 | First race in armour | |
| 490 | | Persians invade Greece<br>Greek victory at Marathon |
| 488 | Miltiades dedicates helmet from Marathon | |
| 484 | Kleomedes kills opponent | |
| 480 | | Persians again invade Greece<br>Greek defeat at Thermopylae |
| | *Themistocles lionized after Salamis* | Greek victories at Salamis and Plataea |
| 478 | | Foundation of Delian League |
| 476 | Theagenes wins pankration<br>Euthymus wins boxing | |
| 472 | | Foundation of democracy of Elis |
| 471 | | Elis wrests control of Games from Pisa |
| 468 | Pherias banned as too young | |
| 464 | Diagoras wins boxing | |
| 462 | | Spartan Helots revolt |
| 458 | Temple of Zeus completed | |

| 448 | Diagoras' sons' victories | |
| 449 | | Peace between Greece and Persia |
| 444 | Taurosthenes wins wrestling | |
| 436 | Pantarkes wins boys' wrestling | |
| | *Herodotus reads* Histories | |
| 433 | | Parthenon completed in Athens |
| 430 | *Statue of Zeus completed* | |
| 431 | | Start of Peloponnesian War |
| 420 | Spartans ban defied by Likhas | Peace of Nikias |
| | Androsthenes wins pankration | |
| 416 | Alcibiades wins chariot race | |
| | Exainetus wins stade race | |
| | Androsthenes wins pankration | |
| 415 | | Athens defeats Melos |
| | | Athenian expedition leaves for Sicily |
| | | Alcibiades defects to Sparta |
| 413 | | Defeat of Athenians in Sicily |
| 412 | Exainetus again wins stade race | 300 chariots escort Exainetus home |
| 411 | | Alcibiades defects to Persia |
| | | Alcibiades rejoins Athenian army |
| 408 | Poulydamas wins pankration | |
| | Archelaos wins chariot race | |
| 406 | | Alcibiades again flees Athens |
| 405 | | Battle of Aigospotamoi |
| 404 | Pherenike exposed as a woman | Defeat of Athens, |
| | | Death of Alcibiades |
| 400 | | *Kreugas killed in boxing at Nemea* |
| 399 | | Socrates executed at Athens |
| 396 | First herald and trumpeter contest | |
| | Kynisca wins chariot race | |
| 390 | *Site of stadium moved out of Altis* | |
| 388 | Eupolus fined for cheating | |
| 360 | *Leonidium Hotel built* | |
| 356 | Philip II wins chariot race | |
| 352 | Philip II wins chariot race | |
| 350 | *Echo Colonnade built* | |
| 348 | Philip II wins chariot race | |
| 338 | *Philippeion built* | Philip II defeats Greeks at Chaironeia |
| 336 | | Alexander the Great assumes power |
| 323 | | Death of Alexander |
| 146 | | Romans sack Corinth |
| 30 | | Roman rule united across Mediterranean |

AD
40   *Caligula tries to remove statue of Zeus*
65   Games postponed to let Nero compete
67   Nero 'wins' ten-horse chariot race
267  Heruli attack Olympia
390  *Statue of Zeus removed to Constantinople*
391                                    Theodosius I bans pagan worship
395-7                                  (?) Visigoths invade Greece
410                                    Alaric sacks Rome
426                                    Theodosius II's decree: destroy temples
462                                    Statue of Zeus destroyed by fire

# WHO'S WHO

Historical characters appear in plain type; *mythological characters in italics;* gods in **bold**

| | |
|---|---|
| *Achilles* | mythical Greek warrior hero of the *Iliad,* friend of Patroclos |
| Aelian | (*c.* AD 175–235) Roman author of *Varia Historia,* a work which includes anecdotes about famous Greek artists, philosophers etc |
| Agesilaus | (444–360 BC; r. 400–360 BC) King of Sparta, brother of Agis II and Kynisca |
| Ageus | winner of the *dolikhos* in 328 BC, ran to Argos the same day with news of his victory |
| Agis II | (r. 427–401 BC) King of Sparta |
| Aglaophon | Athenian painter, his works included a depiction of Alcibiades' chariot victory, which was exhibited on the Athenian Acropolis |
| *Ajax* | mythical Greek warrior hero of the *Iliad* |
| Alaric | (d. AD 410) leader of the Visigoths, sacker of Rome |
| Alexander | (356–323 BC) called 'the Great', King of Macedon, warlord, destroyer of civilizations |
| Alcibiades | (*c.* 450–404 BC) ward of Pericles, Athenian politician and sometime traitor |
| **Alpheios** | local river god |
| *Amycus* | mythical boxer-king of Bithynia |
| Andocides | (440–390 BC) Athenian politician, enemy and prosecutor of Alcibiades |
| Androleus | boxer whose injuries were commemorated in verse |
| Androsthenes | pankratist, winner at Olympia in 420 and 416 BC |
| **Aphrodite** | goddess of sex |
| **Apollo** | god of archery and the arts |
| Archelaos | son of Perdikkas, king of Macedon; winner in the chariot race of 408 BC |
| *Ariadne* | mythical Cretan princess, beloved but abandoned by Theseus |
| Arrhakhion | pankratist, twice winner at Olympia, he died there in 564 BC |
| **Artemis** | goddess of hunting and the wild |

| | |
|---|---|
| **Athene** | daughter of Zeus; goddess of wisdom; patron goddess of Athens |
| Aura | 'Breeze', a mare which won her race without a rider |
| Bacchylides | (b. *c*.510 BC) praise-singer |
| Caligula | (AD 12–41; r. AD 37–41) Roman emperor; tried to move statue of Zeus from Olympia to Rome |
| Chilon | (sixth century BC) Spartan, author of pithy sayings; died at Olympia |
| Clinias | father of Alcibiades |
| Darius | (550–486 BC) Persian Emperor, and unsuccessful invader of Greece |
| **Demeter** | goddess of agriculture and fertility |
| Diagoras | (fifth century BC) boxer and founder of successful boxing dynasty |
| Diognetus | Cretan boxer who killed his opponent at the Olympic Games |
| Diomedes | (fifth century BC) Athenian, erstwhile friend cheated of his chariot by Alcibiades |
| **Dionysus** | god of transformation, wine, drama and fecundity |
| Drakon | (late seventh century BC) Athenian lawgiver |
| Drymos | *dolikhos* winner who ran home to Epidauros to report his victory |
| Epictetus | (AD 55–135) Stoic, if not stoical, philosopher |
| **Eris** | goddess of strife |
| **Eros** | god of sex |
| *Eteokles* | mythical son of Oedipus, died fighting to protect Thebes from his brother's army |
| Euagoras | winner of the first two-horse chariot race at Olympia in 408 BC |
| Eubatas | winner of the stade race at Olympia in 408 BC |
| Eupolus | boxer, Olympia's first cheat, fined in 388 BC for bribing opponents |
| Euripides | (480–406 BC) Athenian playwright; writer of praise-song for Alcibiades |
| Eusebius | (*c*. AD 263–339) Bishop of Caesarea, compiler of Olympic Victors lists |
| Euthymos | boxer, winner at Olympia in 476 BC, vanquisher of the mysterious Hero |
| Glycon | winner of the stade race in 588 BC |
| *Hekabe* | mythical Queen of Troy, heroine of Homer's *Iliad* and Euripides' *Trojan Women* |
| **Hera** | wife of Zeus; patron goddess of the women's festival at Olympia |
| *Heracles* | mythical strongman and accomplisher of many so-called Labours; one of the founders of the Olympic Games |
| Herodotos | (*c*.484–425 BC), 'The Father of History', perhaps read from his account of the Persian Wars in the Temple of Zeus at Olympia |
| Hesiod | (*c*.700 BC?) poet, author of *Theogony* and *Works and Days* |
| **Hestia** | goddess of the hearth |
| Hieron | (d. 467 BC) tyrant of Syracuse, winner of chariot race at Olympia (468 BC) and horse race, commissioner of praise-songs by Pindar and Bacchylides |
| Hippias | (late fifth century BC) polymath from Elis |
| *Hippodameia* | mythical princess, for whose hand Pelops competed against her father |

|  |  |
|---|---|
| | in a chariot race |
| *Hippolytus* | mythical prince of Athens, son of Theseus; died in a chariot accident |
| Homer | (*c.*700 BC?) poet, author of *Iliad* and *Odyssey* |
| Ikkos | pentathlete, Olympic winner (472 BC); first to introduce strict dieting for athletes |
| *Iphitus* | mythical king of Elis, first to award olive crowns at the Games |
| Kallipateira | title given to mother of Pisodorus, a victorious boy-boxer; broke Olympic rules by attending the Games |
| **Kladeos** | local river god |
| Kleomedes | boxer, winner at Olympia in 484 BC; committed school massacre; subsequently heroized |
| Koroibos | runner, winner of the first Olympic stade race in 776 BC |
| **Kronos** | father of Zeus |
| Kynisca | Spartan princess; winner of chariot race in 396 and 392 BC |
| Leonidas | wealthy speculator; builder of first hotel at Olympia |
| Leontiskos | (early fifth century BC) wrestler, specialist in finger-breaking |
| Libon | (mid fifth century BC) architect of Temple of Zeus at Olympia |
| Likhas | Spartan ephor, in 420 BC flouted ban and won chariot race; flogged by Olympic judges |
| Mardonius | (d. 479 BC) Persian general, died at battle of Plataea |
| *Medusa* | mythical gorgon with snake-hair, who could turn mortals into stone |
| Milo | sixth-century BC wrestler and soldier from Croton |
| Miltiades | (*c.*550 – 489 BC) Athenian general, victorious commander at Marathon |
| *Myrtilos* | mythical charioteer, persuaded by Pelops to tamper with Oinomaos' lynchpins |
| **Nemesis** | goddess of retribution |
| Nero | (AD 37–68) Roman emperor, participant in Olympic Games of AD 67 |
| Nikasylos | boy wrestler from Rhodes who competed in the adult category and died before he was 20 |
| Nikias | (*c.*470–413 BC) Athenian politician, engineer of peace with Sparta (421 BC), died fighting in Sicily |
| Nikostratos | winner of the boys' wrestling in 416 BC |
| *Oedipus* | mythical king of Thebes, killer of father; married mother |
| *Oinomaos* | mythical king of Elis, defeated in chariot race by Pelops |
| **Olympia** | the divine personification of the religious site of Olympia |
| Paionios | (late fifth century BC) sculptor of winged Victory at Olympia |
| **Pan** | god of wild places, purveyor of panic |
| Panainos | (late fifth century BC) Athenian painter, brother of Pheidias |
| Pantarkes | (late fifth century BC) boy boxer from Elis, winner at Olympia in 436 BC; lover of Pheidias |
| *Patroklos* | mythical friend of Achilles in *Iliad* |
| Pausanias | (second century AD) traveller, author of *Periegesis* or *Guide to Greece* |
| *Peleus* | mythical king, father of Achilles |

| | |
|---|---|
| *Pelops* | mythical hero, winner of chariot race against Oinomaos, buried at Olympia |
| Perdikkas II | (d. 413 BC) King of Macedon |
| Pericles | (*c*.495–429 BC) Athenian statesman; architect of Athenian Empire Peloponnesian War |
| **Persephone** | daughter of Demeter; like her, a goddess of fertility |
| *Perseus* | mythical hero, slayer of Medusa |
| Pheidias | (late fifth century BC) sculptor of statue of Olympian Zeus and Athene Parthenos, artistic director of Periclean building programme at Athens |
| Pheidolas | Corinthian owner of the mare, Aura |
| Pherenike | aka Kallipateira |
| Pherias | boxer prevented from taking part in Olympic Games of 468 BC because he looked too young |
| Philip II | (382–336 BC) King of Macedon; defeater of Greeks at Chaironeia |
| Philostratus | (AD 170–247) Greek sophist, author of work *On Gymnastics* |
| Pindar | (*c*. 522–443 BC) praise-singer |
| Pisodoros | (fifth century BC) boy boxer, son of Kallipateira |
| Plato | (428–348 BC) Athenian philosopher, pupil and champion of Socrates |
| Plutarch | (*c*. AD 46–120) Greek philosopher and biographer |
| *Polydeuces* | mythical Spartan boxer |
| Polymnestor | (seventh century BC) victor in the boys' stade race |
| *Polyneikes* | mythical brother of Eteokles, died attacking his home city of Thebes |
| Poulydamas | pankratist, winner at Olympia in 408 BC; many legends stem from him |
| *Prometheus* | mythical early mortal, stole fire from gods, cheated them regarding sacrifices |
| Pythagoras | boxer, won at Olympia in 588 BC |
| **Rhea** | wife of Kronos |
| Socrates | (*c*.469–399 BC) Athenian philosopher, friend of Alcibiades |
| Statius | (*c*. AD 45–96) Roman poet |
| *Tantalos* | mythical king punished in the underworld |
| Taurosthenes | wrestler who won at Olympia in 444 BC |
| Thales | philosopher and astronomer who died at Olympia in 548 BC |
| Theagenes | (early fifth century BC) boxer and later hero |
| Themistocles | (*c*.524–459 BC) Athenian politician and general, leader of Greeks at Salamis |
| Theocritus | (third century BC) poet, author of *Idylls* |
| Theodosius I | (AD 347–395) Roman emperor who banned pagan worship |
| Theodosius II | (AD 401–450) Roman emperor who ordered destruction of pagan temples |
| *Theseus* | mythical king of Athens |
| *Thetis* | mythical wife of Peleus and mother of Achilles |
| Thucydides | (*c*.460–400 BC) Athenian general and historian of Peloponnesian War |
| Timanthes | boxer and self-immolator |

| | |
|---|---|
| Timasitheos | wrestler who eventually defeated Milo |
| Woodsman | official at Olympia responsible for provision of poplar wood for sacrifices |
| Xenophon | (c.430–354 BC) Athenian general, historian and author of handbook on equestrianism |
| Xerxes | (519–465 BC) Persian emperor, unsuccessful invader of Greece |
| **Zeus** | king of the gods; patron god of the Olympic Festival |
| Zeuxis | (fifth century BC) artist and self-publicist |

# GLOSSARY

| | |
|---|---|
| Agora | marketplace, commercial and social hub of a town of city |
| Altis | sacred enclosure at Olympia, housing temples, shrines, statues etc |
| Aulos | musical reed instrument family, resembling modern duduk or chanter |
| Balbis | low mound on which discus throwers stood to throw |
| Bouleuterion | Council chamber |
| Centaur | mythical creature, half man, half horse |
| Dithyramb | hymn usually in honour of the god Dionysus |
| Dolikhos | long-distance race over 4614.72 metres |
| Ephor | Spartan magistrate |
| Gymnasium | building complex dedicated to education and athletic training |
| Hellanodikai | judges of the Olympic Games |
| Helot | Spartan slave |
| Hippaphesis | starting mechanism for equestrian races |
| Hippodrome | racetrack for equestrian events |
| Hoplite | heavily armed infantry soldier |
| Hubris | overblown belief in one's superiority, even (at times) to the gods |
| Lapith | mythological tribe which fought the centaurs |
| Metopé | sculptural feature on temples |
| Nemesis | retribution |
| Pantheon | sanctuary dedicated to all the gods (in which sacred olive tree grew) |
| Pelopion | sanctuary to mythical hero Pelops, thought to contain his grave |
| Phthonos | divine anger directed at a mortal guilty of hubris |
| Phyllobolia | ritual of throwing leaves or petals over victorious athletes |
| Prytnaeum | administrative building containing banqueting hall and shrine to Hestia |
| Skamma | landing-pit for long jump |
| Stade | measurement of distance approx 200 metres long; length of foot-race |
| Stadium | venue for foot-races |
| Stoa | colonnaded arcade |
| Taraxippos | altar in the hippodrome noted for frightening the horses |
| Trace horse | The two inner horses in a four-horse team were attached to the chariot yoke; the outer two, the so-called 'trace horses' were attached to the inner horses by bridles. |

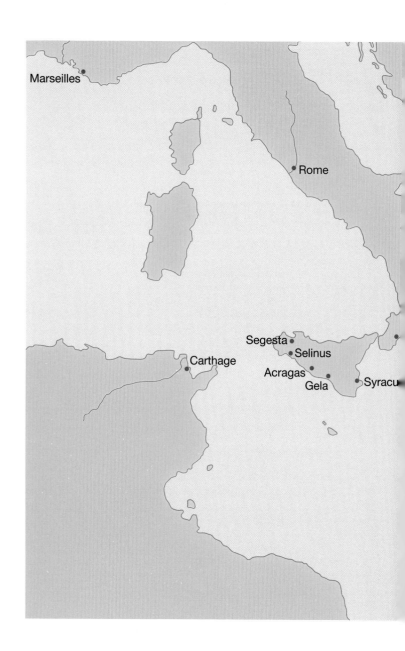

Epidamnus

Macedonia

Thasos

Aigospotamoi

Troy

Constantinople

Lesbos

Delphi

Chios

Sardis

Ephesus

Olympia

Athens

Samos

Ionia

Miletus

Sparta

Delos

Naxos

Melos

Astypalaia

See Map of Greece

Rhodes

Cydonia

Cyrene

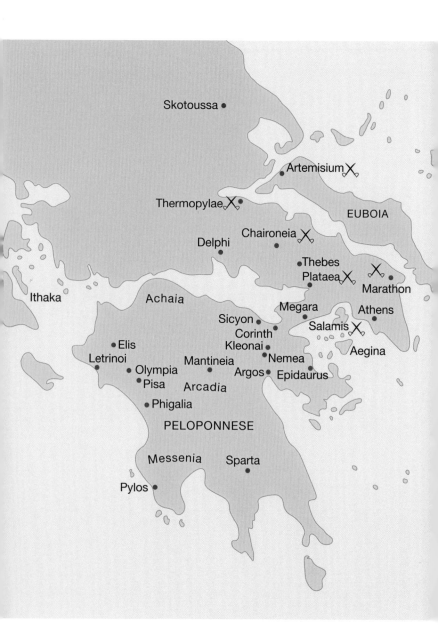

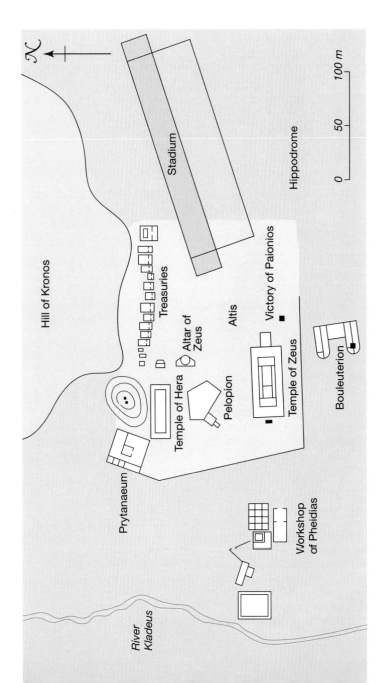

N

0    50    100 m

Hill of Kronos

Stadium

Hippodrome

Treasuries

Altis

Victory of Paionios

Altar of Zeus

Temple of Hera

Pelopion

Temple of Zeus

Bouleuterion

Prytanaeum

Workshop of Pheidias

River Kladeus

# NOTES

Most of the Greek and Roman authors quoted in this text are available in English translations published by Penguin Classics. Unless stated otherwise, all references to Pausanias refer to his *Guide to Greece*, (2 vols) translated by Peter Levi, 1971. Full bibliographical details of the modern works referenced most frequently in these notes can be found on p. 236.

1 Pausanias, 6.20.1

2 See, for example, Swaddling's *The Ancient Olympic Games.*

3 The timing of the festival (like our Easter) varied to ensure it was always in the month corresponding to our August.

4 There was also a festival for women, the Heraia, which included a race, also held every four years, but this book will restrict its scope to the male festival.

5 The so-called Nemean, Pythian and Isthmian Games, which joined with those at Olympia to form a regular circuit.

6 e.g. Pausanias, 5.10.1

7 While the description of the ritual here is speculative, the details of the temple and statue are drawn from literary and archaeological evidence.

8 Olympia itself takes its name from Mount Olympus, many miles distant in north-east Greece. Mount Olympus was the supposed home of the gods, the chief of whom was Zeus. One of his cult titles therefore was Zeus Olympius, or Zeus of Olympus. It is from 'Olympius', that the site of his temple, Olympia, takes its name.

9 The statue of Zeus was begun in *c*.435 BC and finished (perhaps) by 430 BC. See Drees, *Olympia,* pp. 147–149.

10 Pausanias, 5.11.9

11 Pheidias had insisted on installing this black paved area after he saw how the sunlight bouncing onto the statue, from what had been originally a completely white marble floor, caused too much glare.

12 Pausanias (9.41.3) describes the manufacture at Chaironeia in Boeotia of scent from lilies, roses, narcissi and irises. Not only do these scents alleviate human distress, he tells us, but attar of roses rubbed onto statues stops the wood from rotting. The core of Pheidias' statue was, of course, made from wood. Dinsmoor explains: 'oil apparently being necessary to prevent the ivory from splitting, and probably the wooden core from swelling'.

13 Pausanias, 5.11.10

14 He devotes two out of his ten books to Olympia – more than to any other place.

15 The word can also mean 'small figures'.

16 Pausanias, 5.11.1–2 and 7–8

17 Epictetus, *Dissertations*, 2.8.26

18 Epictetus, *Dissertations*, 1.6

19 Hoplites were heavily-armed infantrymen, characterized by their large round shields (*hopla*), which they interlocked to form a tight battle line known as the *phalanx.*

20 It can still be seen in the museum at Olympia.

21 The tent had been left behind by Xerxes when he returned to Persia – it had been inherited by Mardonius.

22 The Helots were the indigenous population who had been enslaved when the early Spartans immigrated into their territory. Kept as farmers and labourers, they were treated with vicious contempt by their Spartan masters.

23 See Sam Moorhead and David Stuttard, 'Riding to resurrection', *British Museum Magazine*, No. 62, Winter 2008.

24 See, for example, Patricia Salzman-Mitchell, 'A whole out of pieces: Pygmalion's ivory statue in Ovid's Metamorphoses', *Arethusa*, Volume 41, Number 2, Spring 2008, pp. 291–311

25 Some of these moulds have been discovered and are in the museum at Olympia.

26 Pausanias, 5.11.3

27 Panainos was either Pheidias' brother or his nephew.

28 Pausanias, 5.11.6. The Painted Stoa was a celebrated colonnade on the north side of Athens' *Agora* (marketplace) adorned with frescoes showing scenes from battles.

29 Homer, *Iliad*, 1.528–530

30 John Grimes Younger, *Sex in the Ancient World from A to Z*, Routledge; Abingdon and New York, 2005, p. 95

31 Pausanias, 5.10.2

32 Epidamnus, also known as Dyrrhachium, modern Durrës in Albania.

33 So called from the Athenians' perspective because most of the city-states against whom they were fighting were located in the southern part of Greece, the Peloponnese. The most famous history of the war was written by Thucydides.

34 See, for example, 'Scientists solve puzzle of death of Pericles', Sarah Boseley, The Guardian, January 24 2006

35 A city on the westernmost prong of the Khalkidike in northern Greece.

36 Opinions are divided as to how long this ban lasted. Some believe that it was not lifted until 400 BC, others that it was for one festival only. The author of the present work tends to this latter view. It should be noted, however, that even if they were banned from competing in the Games, the Spartans were probably allowed to attend the rest of the Festival. After all, even during the ban of 420 BC, Likhas (see Who's Who) was not forbidden from being at Olympia.

37 For a discussion of the Truce see Beale's *Greek Athletics and the Olympics*.

38 Plutarch, *Life of Alcibiades*, 16

39 Plutarch, *Life of Alcibiades*, 9

40 A similar tent was pitched 28 years later by the tyrant Dionysios of Syracuse and described by Diodorus Siculus, 14.109

41 The Eurotas is the river which runs through Sparta.

42 There is limited archaeological evidence of the use of narcotics such as opium in antiquity.

43 Girls married universally and early in classical Greece. In the absence of marriage certificates, the ban on 'married women' must in effect have meant a ban on post-pubescent females.

44 Drees, *Olympia*, p. 57

45 Epictetus, *Dissertations,* 4.4.24

46 Epictetus, ibid., 1.6.23–9. Modern readers may perhaps be reminded of similar discomforts endured by attendees at music festivals such as Glastonbury, where the opportunity to be part of a multitudinous crowd marvelling at a popular rock band is thought by many to outweigh the muddy horrors and their concomitant lack of decent sanitation.

47 The classical Greek day ran from sunset to sunset, not as today from the arbitrary hour of midnight to midnight. We have adhered to the classical pattern in this book, because it makes more sense of the organization of the Games and its events.

48 It is uncertain how many Hellanodikai there were in 416 BC. In 580 BC there were only two, and this may have been the number in 416 BC. By 348 BC the number stood at ten, though between these two dates there had for some time been first nine and then twelve.

49 468 BC

50 Pausanias, 6.14.1

51 ibid.,6.14.2–3

52 Athletes from Athens, for example, might already have taken part in the great procession from that city along the coast to the sacred shrine of Eleusis, and the hallowed mysteries of death and resurrection which were enacted there.

53 Pausanias, 6.26.3

54 ibid., 6.25.1

55 ibid., 6.5.2

56 ibid., 6.16.8

57 It will be recalled that it was with the Month of the Deer (approximately our March) that the Elean year began.

58 This was her *aegis,* the snake-fringed goatskin which Athene wore around her shoulders. In its centre, between Athene's breasts, was the head of the gorgon Medusa, whose glance could turn a man to stone.

59 See Clark, M.,1999 'Thucydides in Olympia' in R. Mellor and L. Tritle (eds.), *Text and Tradition: Studies in Greek History and Historiography in Honor of Mortimer Chambers,* Claremont, California, pp. 115–134

60 Pausanias' tour guide at Olympia assured him (wrongly) that it dated to the early 11th century BC.

61 Pausanias, 5.17.1–3

62 ibid., 5.20.1

63 ibid., 5.20.1–2

64 Apsidal buildings are buildings in which at one end there is a large semicircular recess usually with an arched or domed roof.

65 Pausanias, 5.24.9–11. In the course of this description he adds 'I forgot to ask what they do with the boar after the athletes have taken their oaths. Ancient custom, of course, was that no one should eat any part of an animal over which an oath had been sworn.' Clearly, the wealth of facts with which Olympia and its guides were bombarding him was flustering the usually meticulous Pausanias.

66 Twenty years later, in 396 BC, two new contests were introduced and placed immediately after the oath-taking. These were contests for trumpeters and heralds. When the so-called Echo Colonnade was built (just after 350 BC), the contests were held here because of the taxing acoustics from which it took its name.

67 It was among this 'rubble' that some of the most extraordinary sculptures were subsequently discovered, including the celebrated statue of Zeus and Ganymede.

68 See Drees, *Olympia*, p. 90

69 The stadium was not moved to its present site until the middle of the 4th century BC.

70 Eusebius, *Chronicles*, p. 199

71 The later stadium accommodated twenty runners. Perhaps this was the number entered now. Of course, there had been heats, some when the boys had been in training back in Elis, and weak contestants, not wishing to be shamed, would have dropped out.

72 Pausanias, 1.44.1

73 Philostratos, *On Gymnastics*, 56

74 Sadly, however, it was not to be quite forever, for his name, like that of so many of his sporting colleagues, has not come down to us.

75 See, for example, Aristotle, *Politeia*, 8.4.1 and Philostratus, *On Gym*, 46.

76 Pausanias, 6.14.5

77 Pausanias, 6.14. 6–7

78 Pausanias, 6.14.8

79 Eusebius, *Chronicles*, p. 199

80 Pausanias, 8.26.1

81 The exact location of the contact sports is controversial. For a discussion, see Beale.

82 *Greek Anthology*, 11. 81

83 Pausanias, 5.6.7

84 Plutarch, *Life of Alcibiades,* 9

85 Pausanias, 6.21.9f.

86 Pausanias, 5.17.6

87 Athenaeus, *Banquet of the Sophists*, 205

88 ibid., 412f.

89 *Varia Historia*, 11.3

90 The site of the hippodrome, largely washed away by the flooded river Alpheios, was discovered only in 2008.

91 Built between 466 and 458 BC

92 Pindar, *Olympian*, 3. 33–34

93 Sources are confused about which of the equestrian events came first, but given the Greeks' innate sense of drama, it is likely that they kept the great spectacular of the chariot races until last. Additionally, as has been pointed out by Findlay and Pleket (p. 31, 'riding an unshod horse bareback and without stirrups (neither the horseshoe nor the stirrup was known in antiquity) over a field that had just been churned up by the chariot teams could not have been much fun.'

94 Evidence for this comes from art rather than from literature. Many sculptures show

racehorses ridden by young boys with distinctive African features.

95 The Parthenon Frieze may well demonstrate this link between heroic mortals, horses and a posthumous godlike status. See Moorhead and Stuttard, 'Riding to resurrection', *British Museum Magazine*, No. 62, Winter 2008

96 The two gods, Zeus and Apollo, patrons of the Olympic and Pythian Games respectively, are similarly linked in the sculptures of the east and west pediments of the Temple of Zeus.

97 Pausanias, 6.13.9

98 Euripides, *Hippolytus*, 1. 1233 f.

99 A quarter of a mile

100 Pausanias, 6.20.17. The exact location of the Taraxippos is uncertain and some argue for its being after the turn.

101 The two inner horses in a four-horse team were attached to the chariot yoke; the outer two, the so-called 'trace horses' were attached to the inner horses by bridles.

102 While all classical authors agree that Alcibiades' teams came first and second, Thucydides (*Histories*, 6.16.2) places the next team fourth. Plutarch (*Life of Alcibiades*, 11), however, quotes the Victory Ode, which he attributes to Euripides, as evidence for Alcibiades' chariots having won first, second and third places. In fact, as only the winning team received a prize, the positioning of the others was largely irrelevant.

103 This version is by John Dryden.

104 Athenaeus, *Deipnosophistae*, 12.534D

105 Plutarch, *Life of Alcibiades*, 12

106 Thucydides, ibid.

107 Eight talents: Diodorus, *Historical Library*, 13.74. At this time, a trireme's crew received a combined wage of a talent a month; the maximum length of the sailing season (according to the Roman author Vegetius, *Rei militaris instituta*. 4.3) was from 10th March to 10th October, though more usually it was from 27th May to 14th September.

108 See Chapter 7, page 194.

109 Plutarch, *Life of Agesilaus*, 20

110 Die Inschriften von Olympia (IvO), 160

111 Philostratus, *On Gymnastics*, 31

112 Pausanias, 6.19.1

113 Philostratus the Elder, *Imagines*, 1.24

114 Drees, *Olympia*, p. 74

115 As with much about the pentathlon, there is great debate about exactly how the jump was achieved. For the best summary of ancient evidence, see Beale, *Greek Athletics and the Olympics.*

116 Pausanias, 5.7.10

117 Pindar, *Pythian*, 8.81f.

118 Homer, *Iliad*, 23.

119 Homer, *Iliad*, 23.

120 Pausanias, 5.7.2. A pyre is a structure built of wood for burning the deceased, as part of a funeral rite.

121 i.e. win the favour of

122 Homer, *Odyssey*, 11.20f.

123 Libations were liquid offerings either to the gods or to the dead. Mostly they consisted of wine, or wine mixed with honey.

124 Pausanias, 5.13.3

125 Pindar, *Olympian* 1, 90f.

126 Plutarch, *Life of Alcibiades*, 14 and Andocides, *Against Alcibiades*, 4.30

127 Plutarch, *Life of Alcibiades*, 13 and Andocides, *Against Alcibiades*, 4.29. Andocides, in a speech hostile to Alcibiades, claims that Alcibiades tricked the Athenian authorities into lending him the gold and silverware, keeping it against their wishes to use at the banquet. When it was later used by the city in an official state capacity, many people assumed that it actually belonged to Alcibiades, and that he had allowed Athens to borrow it from him! Tellingly, Andocides claims that some saw the episode as evidence that Alcibiades was showing himself to be superior to his city.

128 Facing ostracism, or expulsion from Athens, the two men had joined forces successfully to diminish a third rival politician.

129 Plutarch, *Life of Alcibiades*, 19

130 Plutarch, ibid.

131 A paean is a song of joyful praise or triumph.

132 Famously, Strife had been overlooked when the wedding guest list had been drawn up, but she attended anyway, bringing with her a golden apple on which was carved the word '*kallistē*', 'to the most beautiful (female) one'. No one was able to agree about who should have the apple, and eventually Zeus passed the decision on to the Trojan prince Paris, who decided in favour of Aphrodite, goddess of sex. As his reward, she gave him Helen, to recover whom the Greeks launched their attack on Troy.

133 See, for example, Drees, *Olympia*, p. 124

134 Pausanias, 5.15.10–11

135 Approximating to our March

136 Pausanias, 5.13.10–11

137 The name used by Pausanias, ibid., for the first level of the altar.

138 Pliny the Elder, *Natural History*, 10.12. Pausanias (5.14.1), however, is more ambiguous, suggesting that it may occasionally have happened that sacrificial meat was indeed snatched by birds of prey.

139 Pausanias, 5.14.1

140 Sacrifice of 100 animals

141 See 'woodsman', page 221.

142 The stade takes under 30 seconds to run; the actual religious or ritual significance of the race, however, was undoubtedly much greater.

143 See, for example, Finlay and Pleket, *The Olympic Games*, p. 25

144 Eusebius himself appears to have taken much of the details of the Olympic victors lists from Sextus Julius Africanus, a fellow Christian of the early third century AD, who chronicled the history of the world from its creation (by his calculations this took place in 5500 BC) to his own day.

145 Philostratus, *Lives of the Sophists*, 1.11.1

146 Plato, *Hippias Minor*, 360D.ff.

147 4614.72 metres to be precise, so a similar distance to the modern 5,000-metre race. The longer marathon race is, of course, a modern invention, introduced at the Athens Games of AD 1896.

148 Such were the ideal characteristics of the *dolikhos* runner, according to Philostratus, *On Gymnastics*, 32

149 Drees, p. 80

150 Statius, *Thebaid*, 6.587ff.

151 In Pausanias' day (second century AD) it appears that these heats were run off on the same day as the final stade race (6.13.4 – a sadly corrupt passage). We do not know when or where the heats were run in 416 BC. It may be that they had already been held before the start of the Games proper at Elis.

152 Both Plutarch and Herodotus recount the story of how, before the Battle of Salamis, Themistocles was threatened with a beating by the Spartan admiral Eurybiades, who chided him for his impetuosity, reminding him that runners who started too soon were similarly punished. Themistocles famously replied: 'Yes, but those who are too slow don't win a crown.' (Plutarch, *Life of Themistokles*, 2 and Herodotus, *Histories*, 8.59)

153 Statius, ibid.

154 Homer, *Iliad*, 23.759ff.

155 Modern Agrigentum in Sicily

156 Diodorus Siculus, *Historical Library*, 13.82.7

157 Hesiod, *Theogony*, 536ff.

158 Pre-pubscent of course.

159 A stringed instrument of ancient Greece belonging to the harp family, with two curved arms connected by a yoke from which strings are stretched to the body. The lyre was used to accompany singing and recitation.

160 (Pseudo) Plato in *The Lovers* (136) remarks that Pentathletes are inferior to specialist wrestlers.

161 Pausanias, 6.14.6ff.

162 Philostratus, *On Wrestling*, 35, describes the ideal wrestler predictably enough – broad shoulders, strong chest, muscular arms and thighs. More surprising is his insistence on the wrestler possessing good buttocks and his reflection that 'well-formed buttocks are an asset for everything'.

163 This also happened if an athlete found himself unmatched in the first round, because there was an odd number of entrants. Then, he too would automatically go through. It would have been extremely humiliating for a wrestler to back out at Olympia itself, especially as they would have had time to evaluate their opponents during the training month at Elis. Perhaps such stories as we have refer to athletes pulling out during this training period.

164 Swaddling, p. 73

165 Pausanias (6.4.3f.) saw his statue, ascribed to the fifth-century artist Pythagoras of Rhegium, who was, he said, 'as good a sculptor as has ever been'. There are those

who claim that the Delphic Charioteer is his work.

166 POxy, 3.466.2

167 Pausanias, 6.9.3

168 Aelian, *Varia Historia*, 9.2

169 Philostratus, *On Gymnastics*, 34

170 Theokritos, *Idylls*, 22.44f.

171 around 400 BC

172 Pausanias, 8.40.5

173 Photius, *Codex*, 190

174 Pausanias, 6.9.6

175 Pausanias, 6.8.4

176 Pausanias, 6.6.7ff.

177 Pausanias, 6.6.11

178 See, for example, Sophocles, *Oedipus at Kolonos*, lines 1655ff.

179 Pausanias, 6.7.3

180 Plutarch, *Life of Pelopidas*, 34 – in other words, 'you have reached the peak of human achievement – only by becoming a god (which you cannot do) could you be any greater'.

181 Aulus Gellius, *Attic Nights*, 3.15.3

182 See, for example, Herodotus, *Histories*, 1.31

183 Plutarch, *Life of Alcibiades*, 2

184 Philostratus, *Pictures in a Gallery*, 2.6

185 Pausanias, 8.40.1

186 Pausanias, 6.11.2f (first quote) and ibid., 6.11.6 (second quote)

187 ibid.

188 Pausanias, 6.5.1ff.

189 Plutarch, *Life of Alcibiades*

190 Philostratus, *On Gymnastics*, 32–33, recommended that runners in this race should have long waists, muscular shoulders and upward titling knees, to help … facilitate the carrying of the shield.

191 Greaves were armour for the legs.

192 Pausanias, 5.8.10

193 Philostratus, *On Gymnastics*, 7

194 Herodotus, *Histories*, 6

195 Pindar, *Isthmian*, 1.50–1

196 i.e. roughly 400 metres. See Pausanias, 2.11.8 and 10.34.5

197 Thucydides, *Histories*, 5.105

198 See also *Trojan Trilogy* reconstructed by David Stuttard, 2007.

199 Bacchylides, *Epineikioi*, 7.10f.

200 Scholars debate whether the ceremony took place inside or just outside the temple; there is not enough evidence to be certain either way.

201 See Spivey, p. 130 and Pindar, *Olympian*, 9.1f.

202 Pausanias, 5.20.1

203 Pausanias, 5.15.3

204 Scholium on Pindar's *Olympian*, 3.60

205 Phlegon of Tralles in Jacoby *Fragmente griechister Historiker*, No. 257, Fragment 12

206 Rodenwaldt, *Olympia*, pp. 21–22

207 Indeed, there is even some contradictory evidence suggesting that in at least one period of the Games the olive wreaths may have been awarded to the athletes immediately after their contest was finished. On balance, it is likely, however, that in 416 BC there was some sort of ceremony such as that which is described here.

208 Hieron of Syracuse in 476 BC

209 Bacchylides, *Epinician Odes*, 5.16f.

210 Lucian, *In Defence of Statues*, 11, has this on hearsay; besides, he is writing in the second century AD, so the rule may not have applied in 416 BC.

211 The celebrated Delphic Charioteer comes from such a statue group (and has influenced this description), as do the four bronze horses now on the balcony of the Basilica of St. Mark, in Venice.

212 Pausanias, 6.12.1

213 Pindar, *Isthmian*, 4 str. 3

214 Bacchylides, *Epinician Odes*, 5.37f.

215 Market square

216 Pausanias, 8.36.8

217 This reconstruction is based on that contained in Drees (p. 106) which itself follows the 'almost entirely hypothetical' account in Mezö's *Geschichte der Olympischen Spiele*, Munich 1930. There is much in Mezö's account which is eminently plausible, and we should not let the date and place of the publication of his work (in Germany in the years preceding the Nazification of the Berlin Games) stop us from following his instinctual lead.

218 Council chamber

219 So conjectures Drees, p. 85

220 Pausanias, 5.15.12

221 Pliny, *Natural History*, 35.36

222 Diogenes Laertius, *Lives of Eminent Philosophers*, 1.68–73

223 ibid., 1.10–12. Note that Diogenes Laertius does not state that his death was at Olympia.

224 Thucydides, *Histories*, 3.14

225 ibid., 3.16

226 Andocides, *Against Alcibiades*, 22

227 Thucydides, *Histories*, 6.6

228 Behaviour which steps beyond the bounds of what is acceptable for a human.

229 See Stuttard, *An Introduction to Trojan Women*, Company Dionysus, 2005

230 Herodotus, *Histories*, 1.87

231 Thucydides, 6.15

232 There is some confusion whether the chariots came first, second and fourth or first, second and third.

233 Thucydides, *Histories,* 6.16

234 Plutarch, *Life of Alcibiades*, 4

235 These may have been the same state cups which Alcibiades had used for his banquet at the Olympic Festival only the year before.

236 Thucydides, *Histories,* 6.32

237 ibid., 6.27f.

238 Plutarch, *Life of Alcibiades*, 23

239 To say that the Spartan constitution was eccentric would be an understatement. Two kings ruled jointly, usually one was responsible for home affairs, the other for war.

240 The five ephors or 'overseers' wielded great power in Sparta – even greater than that of the kings, who were answerable to them. Only at The Edinburgh Academy is the word now common in Britain, where it is the term used for a prefect.

241 Such is the view of Donald Kagan, *The Peloponnesian War*, 282–3

242 Thucydides, 6.90–1

243 Thucydides, 8.9–10

244 Plutarch, *Life of Alcibiades*, 23

245 Aristophanes, *Lysistrata*, 1128ff. (adapted); see (ed) Stuttard, *Looking at Lysistrata*, p. 6

246 Plutarch, *Life of Alcibiades*, 36

247 ibid., 39

248 ibid.

249 i.e. The more substantial parts of the tented city.

250 Xenophon, *Hellenica*, 7.4.28–32

251 Pausanias, 5.20.4. In the omitted sentence, Pausanias mistakes the battle in which the soldier fell, saying it was during the war between the Eleans and the Spartans.

252 82 metres to be exact. Michael Scott (*Delphi and Olympia*, Cambridge University Press 2010, p.187) has recently argued that the relocation of the stadium took place somewhat earlier (at the same time as the construction of the Temple of Zeus). However, he maintains that the embankment, which formed a physical barrier between the temple and stadium, was not built until the fourth century BC.

253 Instituted in 396 BC

254 Pausanias, 5.21.17

255 80 metres x 74 metres, to be exact.

256 Suetonius, *Life of Nero*, 24.2

257 The statue now in the Olympia Museum bears all the hallmarks of a Hellenistic or Roman copy. Pausanias (5.17.3) believed that he saw the genuine statue. Perhaps he did and it was removed after his time.

258 See Moorhead and Stuttard, *AD 410, The Year that Shook Rome*, The British Museum Press, 2010

259 Suetonius, *Caligula*, 57

260 This patrician (or aristocrat) was a wealthy Greek man called Lausus.

# FURTHER READING

A large number of books are available on the ancient Olympic Games and on athletics in antiquity. Of the following, all are recommended.

Beale, A., *Greek Athletics and the Olympics*, Cambridge University Press, 2011
Drees, L., *Olympia*, Pall Mall Press, 1968
Finley, M.I. and Pleket H.W., *The Olympic Games*, Dover Publications Inc, 2009
Miller, S.G., *Arete, Greek Sports from Ancient Sources*, University of California Press, 2004
Spivey, N., *The Ancient Olympics*, Oxford University Press, 2004
Swaddling, J., *The Ancient Olympic Games*, British Museum Press, 2011

# AUTHOR'S ACKNOWLEDGEMENTS

Athletes in the ancient Greek Olympics undoubtedly relied on a team of expert coaches and trainers to support them on their path to competition. Likewise, this book would never have crossed the finishing line of publication without the generous help and backing of a dedicated group of colleagues and friends.

I am hugely grateful to Naomi Waters, Commissioning Manager at the British Museum Press and to Rosemary Bradley, Director of Publishing for supporting the book's commissioning; to Axelle Russo for helping track down images; to Zoë Mellors for her excellent design; to David Hoxley for his splendid maps; to the British Museum's Department of Photography and Imaging for providing such a treasure trove of wonderful images; and to Sarah Morgan for promoting the book with mastery, bravura and aplomb.

My heartfelt thanks go to my editor, Emma Poulter, for her patience, professionalism and calm perseverance, which made the process of writing and refining so much more agreeable.

Thanks also to Sam Moorhead and Alan Beale for their kindness in reading the text, for making such perceptive comments and for giving such invaluable advice. Any shortcomings that remain are entirely my own responsibility.

Finally, I would like to thank friends and family (my mother, Kate, especially) for their tremendous support and encouragement. But, the greatest thanks of all goes to my wife, EJ, without whom, in all honesty, this book would never have been written. Like Heracles, shown labouring on the metopés of Zeus' temple, always aware of Athene's guiding power and presence, I have forever been bolstered by EJ's strength and wisdom. She is truly deserving of an olive crown.

# PICTURE CREDITS

Except for the image on p. 32, all images illustrating objects are © The Trustees of the British Museum. The British Museum registration numbers for these objects are given below. The image on p. 213 and all of the site photographs featured in this book are © David Stuttard.

The image on p. 32 is © akg-images / John Hios.

# MUSEUM REGISTRATION NUMBERS

| | | | |
|---|---|---|---|
| 2 | CM 1841,0726.288 | 123 | GR 1856,1001.1 |
| 20 | GR 1837,0609.59 | 124 | GR 1837,0609.69 |
| 28 | GR 1816,0610.19 | 126 | GR 1837,0609.69 |
| 43 | GR 1856,0902.63 | 132–3 | GR 1848,0619.7 |
| 44 | GR 1873,0820.31 | 136 | GR 1900,1213.1 |
| 46 | GR 1816,0610.11 | 138 | GR 1867,0508.968 |
| 50–1 | GR 1896,0615.1 | 141 | GR 1873,0820.371 |
| 52 | GR 1905,0126.1 | 142 | GR 1843,1103.69 |
| 58 | GR 1867,0508.1119 | 145 | GR 1814,0704.569 |
| 61 | GR 1864,1007.156 | 146 | GR 1873,0820.370 |
| 64 | GR 1836,0224.196 | 151 | GR 1850,0302.2 |
| 69 | GR 1850,0302.2 | 157 | GR 1814,0704.1206 |
| 72 | GR 1880,1211.1 | 158 | GR 1848,0801.1 |
| 75 | GR 1849,0623.48 | 162 | GR 1824,0497.21 |
| 76 | GR 1925,0422.1 | 165 | GR 1843,1103.53 |
| 79 | GR 1836,0224.191 | 170–1 | GR 1816,0610.42 |
| 80 | GR 1836,0224.192 | 172 | GR 1849,1122.1 |
| 82–3 | GR 1816,0610.47 | 175 | GR 1874,0710.347 |
| 84–5 | GR 1866,0415.249 | 176 | GR 1894,0718.7 |
| 86 | GR 1836,0224.179 | 189 | GR 1867,0508.963 |
| 88–9 | GR 1856,1226.1 | 192 | GR 1805,0703.24 |
| 94–5 | GR 1837,0609.69 | 197 | GR 1848,1020.35 |
| 96–7 | GR 1847,0806.26 | 200 | GR 1866,1201.1028 |
| 99 | GR 1892,0718.9 | 202 | CM 1919,0820.1 |
| 100 | GR 1843,1103.14 | 206 | GR 1856,1226.779 |
| 108 | GR 1892,0518.1 | 210 | CM BNK,R.13 |
| 110 | GR 1971,1101.1 | | |
| 114 | GR 1816,0610.9 | | |
| 118–19 | GR 1805,0703.307 | | |

# INDEX